Laid Off & Loving It!

How People Like You
Conquered A Career Crisis

Paul David Madsen
AmericasJobCoach.com ™

Including:

The Twenty-Minute Career Tune-Up ™

&

101+ Career-Enhancing Internet Links

First Edition—Release 1.0

growmedia.com, Omaha, Nebraska U.S.A.

Laid Off & Loving It!
How People Like You
Conquered A Career Crisis

By: Paul David Madsen

Published by:
  Growmedia.com
  12105 West Center Road   Suite 246
  Omaha, NE 68144   U.S.A.

orders@americasjobcoach.com
www.AmericasJobCoach.com

This publication is designed to provide accurate and authoritative information with regard to the subject matter covered. It is published and sold with the agreement that the author and the publisher are not engaged in rendering legal, accounting or other professional advice. If legal advice or other expert assistance is required, the services of a competent professional person should be sought.

Copyright © 2001 by Paul David Madsen

Library of Congress Cataloging-in-Publication Data

Madsen, Paul David.
      Laid Off & Loving It! How People Like You Conquered A
      Career Crisis
      by Paul David Madsen
      Includes Biographical references
      ISBN 0-9713836-0-X
      1.   Careers. 2. Employment 3. Small Business
      II. Title.
      2001118687   CIP

Why This Book Can Help You

For most people, a career crisis can be among the most stressful of life events. Finances and self-esteem are bruised and bloodied. The pressure builds because we live in a changing world. Today, the search for relevant answers to career questions and dilemmas through the use of conventional wisdom and traditional solutions often leads to disappointment. What to do?

We attempt to navigate the ladder of success in an age when job security is nothing more than illusion. Like a mirage in the desert, positions and careers vanish with little notice. The reality of work life today is that security and risk have become so compressed that it's difficult to recognize one from the other.

In this volatile environment, we must focus on what we *can* control. Making appropriate occupational choices is fundamental to success, but frequently difficult. Whether laid off or unhappily employed, you stand at the crossroads of two divergent journeys. One road is traditional and well worn, the other progressive, sophisticated and personal. Choosing the first highway might get you a job. Venturing down the road less traveled can provide fulfillment and meaning.

You have taken the customary route before. Resumes, cover letters, networking, job fairs, online searches, and phone calls. You know when you "arrive" because you end up with a job offer, but you are not sure how you got there *or even if you want to be there.*

There is nothing mystical or obscure about an alternate route, but it does require plans and processes that are not self-evident. To implement this new strategy, you will need a guide. My strong recommendation is Career

Laid Off & Loving It!

Coach, Headhunter, and Employment Specialist Paul David Madsen, C.P.C.

Mr. Madsen is supremely qualified for the task. I first crossed paths with Paul in the early days of our careers when we were employed at an executive search firm. Even then, it was clear that Paul had great enthusiasm for the employment services sector. Specifically, it was clear then, as it is now, that Paul has both a deep passion and skill for enabling the occupational successes of others.

Paul has gained a diverse, in-depth understanding of the employment landscape. Years of executive recruiting, contract placement, out-placement and career coaching experience give Paul insight and perspective. He has personally been involved with the successful career transitions of hundreds of job seekers, career changers, seminar attendees, and individual coaching clients.

Libraries are laden with stuffy "How To" books that are rarely read. *Laid Off & Loving It!* though, teaches without being preachy or academic. Through a series of concise, inspirational narratives, you will learn how others like you have solved their own career crises. Later, you are provided with a nuts-and-bolts framework for forward movement in your own exciting occupational journey.

Will your business or job make something for you or will it make something *of* you? The relevance and value of achieving a thing is not so much in attainment of the goal, but rather in what we must become to make it happen. What do you want to become? My friend Paul David Madsen's book will empower you to *define and obtain YOUR occupational desires*.

Curt McLey, CPC
CEO, Harrison Moore, Inc.
& Long-Time Radio Personality

4

Introduction

Are you a victim or a victor? Everyone who does some form of work for some form of compensation WILL encounter changes in their work life. Why? Because occupations involve customers, co-workers, bosses, competitors, procedures, changing markets, egos, and money. These ingredients often prove to be a volatile mixture. The US Department of Labor states that at least 3,300,000 people are laid off each and every year!

Cement cutters, CEOs, and most workers in between regularly experience life-changing career events. Career change is the norm in corporate America because layoffs, downsizing, re-engineering, discrimination, worker performance, health issues, mergers, and business closings are a regular part of the scene. Employees and employers alike are affected radically by these changes. These stories chronicle the events of how people like you handle workplace transitions.

In a period of twelve years I was laid off three times but this book is not about me. Instead, it describes the actions and thought processes that others applied as they conquered *their* career crises. A few workers sail smoothly from promotion to promotion and retire happily ever after. But, after personally interviewing over 18,000 professionals, I know firsthand that only a few people accomplish that kind of feat. This book is for the rest of us who may need a guiding example when those inevitable "career speed bumps" occur.

Some of the career lessons within are obvious and some are subtle. Each chapter contains nuggets that can apply to you. Even if you do not have the same background as the person in one of the chapters, you *can* learn from their successful transitions. Their stories can still be helpful to you during your own occupational setbacks, career crisis, or event. If, while reading this book, you say: "I could never do that" or, "That's not realistic for me;" then consider what your personal reality IS. Are there any other ways of looking at your world? Do you need to change your point of view in order to conquer events that are affecting you? What part of each person's story can be a positive example for you?

This book then, reflects real life: You have the exciting opportunity to choose your own response to your evolving occupational situation. Will you be a victim or a victor?

Also, we are interested in hearing YOUR story. Please visit our web site (www.americasjobcoach.com) to learn how your story can be part of our future books on occupational life transitions.

The greatest good you can do for another is not just to share your riches, but to reveal to him, <u>his own</u>.

Benjamin Disreali

Table of Contents

Acknowledgements

These stories of occupational inspiration come from the career tales of thousands of people I have met, studied, interviewed, and worked with over nearly two decades in the employment services and executive recruiting sector. Being a recruiter for that long has enabled me to see all sides of career success and failure. I thank all of you who have allowed me to be part of your occupational journeys.

My occupational story happens to include this book because of the encouragement many of you have given me along the way. Thanks to the following for their encouragement and support: Jennifer J. Jensen, Curt McLey, Susan Thaden, Marilyn Arnold, and Cris Moore. Thanks also to Michelle Mahowald for proofreading and especially Lynn Miles Harlow for her excellent editing skills. And thanks to the many seminar attendees who encouraged me to write this book.

Special appreciation goes to my father, Lester Madsen. He was a wordsmith who influenced me in many positive ways. And thanks to Laura, Barb, Dave, Verlan, and Helga for always listening. Finally, special thanks to my family, Lisa, Laura, Dane, and Jake who support me with love, time, and belief. Together we **are** adding value to others!

1

Changing Uses Changes Value

CEO Harry Now Hunts Heads

Harry the CEO was let go after 18 years with his firm. He started there right after college graduation, landing a sales job. He went on to enjoy a great climb to the top in this "first-mover" telemarketing firm.

That early-mover advantage enabled the company to grow to over 2,800 employees at fourteen call centers in six states. There were only sixty-two employees on board when Harry signed on. Phone-based, inbound and outbound sales and customer support were becoming the business norm for many corporations who outsourced these functions to companies like Harry's.

Harry regularly brought in new, high profile clients, projects and accounts. His promotion to sales manager was logical. He enrolled in and completed his evening/weekend MBA program. After closing even more new major accounts, and adeptly playing company politics, Harry was promoted to the VP of Sales.

Harry's passion for the company ran deep and he became friends with the founder. He created a legendary sense of community within his sales staff and these efforts paid off. The company had become positioned for an IPO, which occurred smoothly. Harry's net worth grew significantly.

Mentoring and coaching from outside executives helped Harry to continue up his fast track. His sales organization drove even more revenues. Harry had become the company's "golden child" and he worked about seventy-five hours a week. He actively studied the operations, finance, HR, and production sides of the house and became recognized as an expert in the industry.

As the founder lost interest in running the day-to-day operations, Harry's name naturally surfaced as the replacement and he was appointed CEO. He enjoyed a large salary, travel perks, performance incentives, stock, and all that came with the brass ring. He savored the admiration of his peers, the national recognition, and this ultimate endorsement of his hard work and proven expertise.

It was fun for Harry to see how doors opened for him due to his new title. He had maintained and managed his own rapidly growing personal contacts database since he was a rookie. As a CEO, his personal and professional contacts grew even more rapidly—now totaling over 6,000 contacts. As the top dog, Harry made key staffing actions and put his personal stamp on the operation. Under this leadership, the company chugged away, and earned steady profits.

After seven years as CEO, Harry's marketplace changed. The Internet became the new buzzword in the direct marketing world. Public sentiment against telemarketing was growing and Congress was even considering restrictive laws. Wall Street analysts punished Harry's firm for not being on top of these trends and its stock sank.

The founder's nephew, who was also on the board of directors, talked endlessly about the "New Net Economy." With an eye on Harry's job, he persuaded the board to dump their "relic" of a

CEO. Years of steady profits meant nothing in the face of amazing Internet IPO stories. While he was bitter at first, Harry understood how this had occurred, and vowed to learn from it. The sting of his slapped ego was dulled by a severance package equal to one year of compensation.

Harry traveled, golfed, and finally kept his dates with his special friend, Barb. After four months off, though, Harry was ready to get back in the hunt. Headhunters called but most of them discussed jobs that were lesser to his previous one.

During a visit with one executive recruiter, Harry became intrigued with that profession. Success therein appeared to be based on one's ability to network and introduce the right players to each other at the right time. Harry had the sales ability and contacts—he just needed specific industry content expertise. He obtained that by retaining a top trainer in the executive search industry.

Harry chose to go solo in his recruiting practice. He knew he could learn from others, but he also knew that he was a quick study and very well connected. He relished his quiet office where he made many new and legacy contacts each day. Utilizing his personal database, Harry felt like an account executive again—only now he possessed an influential peer network. His former peers and coworkers seemed jealous of Harry's work hours and the fact that he had no direct reports, board of directors, or shareholders.

Harry placed six executives in his first year—five at firms where he knew people, and one that represented a new client relationship. His average fee was over $37,000. This revenue did not match his former comp plan, especially since he now had expenses. But, the money was in the ballpark and there was a tremendous, upside potential.

Now Harry selects his own hours and projects. He feels poised to grow revenues by at least 50% in his second full year. He became engaged to Barbara and is building his position as a headhunting leader in his niche. Harry rarely misses those hectic days when he was a CEO.

Web Sites That Were Helpful to Harry:

www.napc.org
National Association of Personnel Consultants

www.tpetra.com
Recruiting Industry Trainer

www.ypo.org
Support Organization for Young CEOs/Presidents

www.411web.com
American Teleservices Association (trade group)

www.lycos.net-temps.com
click on "executive" for C-Level postings

2

Use Your Connections

Venture Vicki Connects

My college major was sales and marketing because I have been a persuasive person all of my life. I sold more Girl Scout cookies than anyone in my suburb and the big tip money I earned from my paper routes and waitress jobs gave me a "tax problem" while I was still a teenager. Mom is the real extrovert, so I "blame" her for my outgoing nature.

My first post-college job was selling for a health-care products company. My customers were clinics, doctor's offices, and hospitals. After just two years, I became the best producer company-wide for our regional firm. I declined a promotion to sales manager as I didn't want to baby-sit unmotivated peers, fill out reports for half the day in a cubicle, nor was I interested in a pay cut. I was born to manage and build my own territory. I made nearly $134,000 in year three. Not bad money for that "loudmouth girl from the suburbs!"

Then Dad's prediction came true. He had said that many successful sales reps end up getting their territory cut and my turn for that had now arrived. My employer pulled a couple of key accounts away and told me to go find new customers "just like" those primary accounts. For a sales company they sure were stupid about selling. The fact was that I had I made those customers into key accounts! I hunted and farmed all of the relationships at those companies and turned them into the trophies that they now were!

Now they want to hand my trophies over to a marginal rep or a new kid who has done nothing to earn it? Give me a break!! Because I had $32,000 in liquid savings and investments I promptly quit. They begged me to come back but my pride was hurt. They were a great first job but **I had outgrown them**. Plus, I wanted to check out the e-business buzz.

My next job was with a firm that planned to revolutionize the travel industry since it was anticipated that everyone would use our Internet based business travel services. I was told that we had high-powered angels who invested "millions." I also heard that "venture capital firms were knocking at our door to hand us more money." It all sounded very exciting and I accepted an offer that included thousands of stock options.

My job would be to sell our B2B services to the C-level executives at mid-sized companies. I managed to close some initial deals with clients. The dollar volume of my sales was not huge, but it kept our investors hopeful and they communicated their approval of my work.

By accident, I became a student of the venture capital financing game. I was appointed as the secondary contact person, supporting out CFO's contact with the VC firm. Our CFO traveled heavily, so I was often gathering and communicating financial information. Our financial officer walked me through the steps many times. Everyone liked the way I handled our investment partners.

When the dot-com crash hit, I was asked to remain on board because the owners liked my savvy and the relationships I had established with our investors. They thought that they were going to be able to get another round of financing but I knew

17

that would not happen. I bolted from that company and scheduled lunch appointments with my VC friends.

When I told Daniel that I wanted to join his VC firm, he explained the credentials of the people who he worked with. They *all* had tremendous backgrounds including MBAs, PhDs, and years of M & A, and investment banking experience. My BS degree and a few years of selling couldn't get me in their door. Still, I pointed out to him that his biggest business problem was a shortage of *solid* potential deals. He agreed but he still couldn't hire me.

That conversation set me thinking about the need for "bird-dogs" in that field. After hours of library, Internet, and telephone research, I decided to form my own "bird dog" agency that introduced emerging companies, "certified," high-net-worth individuals, and investment bankers to each other.

I could try this because failing wouldn't be the end of the world. I could always go get a job selling somewhere. I had little overhead or debt, my current wardrobe was appropriate, and I could office out of my apartment's second bedroom. My fast Internet connection and the second phone line covered me and I owned a hot portable computer.

I planned on a slow ramp-up, so I cut back on my living costs— except my sports car. It was part of the image I wanted to portray to my clientele – fast, expensive, successful. My parents gave me a loan to help out with my first year operating and living expenses. They thought I should take another sales job, but history was on my side. They had watched me succeed in ventures since age seven.

I was a fish out of water at first, but nobody could canvas a territory like me. I steadily found, approached, and pre-qualified several start-ups, high net-worth individuals, and VC firms interested in doing deals. The hardest part was finding the high net worth investors who would chat with me about possibly becoming an investor. But, I worked very hard, did some awesome networking and my word-of-mouth referrals spread.

The investment banking firms were skeptical of me at first since I was an outsider. But I reeled them in because I approached them with potential deals. Results get attention. I kept focused on being the person to bring them new, viable prospects. And they should be open-minded to me—my services were free! I just get a tiny finder's fee for each deal they actually chose to facilitate.

Two mid-level prospects that I brought to the VC firms were eventually funded. One was an investor who put forth some major funding and the other was an emerging company that got funded. Each deal put thousands of dollars into my pocket. I continue a blistering pace of phone work, lunches, and social/civic events. I have meaningful telephone conversations with forty-some people a day and I love the action! Even in periods of investor caution, I can dig out and find emerging companies or ready investors. And this has proven to be of value to the venture firms that I have targeted.

I love life because I now feel like I am in control of my own territory, time, and earnings. My skill rewards me instead of others and I am building a good name for myself. Next year, I hope to double my number of finder's fee deals!

Web Sites That Were Helpful To Vicki:

www.nvca.com
National Venture Capital Association

www.cvca.com
Canadian Venture Capital Association

www.moneyhunter.com
Program introducing investors to investments

www.sba.gov/womeninbusiness
Federal Small Business Administration

3

Nurture Your Connections

Meal-Man Mike Caters To Executives

Here is the story of how I got my business started. You asked for a lot of detail so I gave you all the ingredients!

Mike

Catering Business Journal

I have fifteen years of food service experience at age thirty because I started in food service when I was only fifteen years old. I worked up to thirty-hours per week during high school. I was never into sports, music or drama and my family liked it when I brought home a paycheck. Plus, the other co-workers at my fast-food employers became my social group. The three different franchised food operations I worked for while in high school were similar but different. I changed jobs for better pay and I learned more at each employer.

By the time I graduated, my manager wanted me to join his store as an assistant manager trainee. I knew most production tasks but not the finance side of the business. Also, I had no

"HR" experience other than training of dozens of new workers. I signed on and also pursued the food services program at our community college. It taught me both the business elements and the technical, "art" side of food preparation. I earned a near-perfect GPA. I worked full time and was a full time student so I had no life!

Upon graduation, I signed on as Assistant Manager with an upscale restaurant here in town. We offered "a unique and excellent dining experience" to our guests and that was a fun switch. It was a different life than the franchise world because an interesting local woman owned it. It was a very personable place and she knew many of her regular customers. I too got to know her and often picked her brain regarding the restaurant business. I took on more responsibility over the next three years, but there was no upward mobility for me there because we were a one-store operation. My manager made great money and he was not going anywhere soon. My earnings were great too but I was restless.

I ended up landing a position as the store manager of another upscale, casual dining café with an ethnic flavor. I joined them because they had twelve full-service restaurants, assuring future upward mobility. This place was a similar to my former employer—quality food, an upbeat staff, great money, and lots of hours. But this was my best employer yet because it where I met Cindy. She was a part-time waitress and college student. After we became "an item," I avoided any preferential treatment of her and kept things very professional at the restaurant. Only her close friends knew we were dating. We were married a year later.

At twenty-five, I became the youngest regional manger this restaurant group had ever had. I managed store managers who were ten years senior to me. Most of my stores built prof-itability over time but turnover of good managers was always a problem. I ended up conducting much weekend training of new managers.

21

After three years, I learned about a job at a local country club. They needed a manager for their bar and restaurant operation. I was happy with my present job but I had heard that the pay at the club was outstanding. Plus, I decided that I wanted to stop running around to several stores and just go to one location again. We had a two-year-old and another baby on the way.

The new club offered the best service, quality, and clientele. I thrived and excelled at staff training, menu additions, service improvement, and everything else. The club manager was very pleased at how I extended the sales in several areas. The most fun for me was getting to know the regular customers. "Relational sales" helped me meet lots of well-connected people.

After about a year, a member who was the Chief Operating Officer for a large insurance company struck up a conversation with me about my career. He explained that his company had just lost their Director of Food Services and he was interested in having me run his employee cafeteria and executive dining room. That kind of work didn't appeal to me since I was an "upscale" manager now. But, he lured me away with the idea that I would have a "Director" title in a major corporation, more pay, and better fringe benefits for my family. He closed me when he explained that there would be virtually NO weekend work!

Corporate life was a different world. The executive and employee dining rooms were not profit centers, so I had to fight for budget money to make improvements. Raising prices significantly was not an option. I made some cosmetic changes that were well received, but I was a fish out of water. I did enjoy meeting and catering to the executives though. I got to know most of them well because they welcomed my "food events."

After eighteen boring months, the insurance firm brought in a nationally managed food service contractor that promised savings. Perhaps their economies of scale could cut costs and maintain quality but I didn't buy it. They promised me a job, but at a reduced pay scale with poorer fringe benefits. I quit. Since age fifteen, I had worked too many hours to become much of a spender. With the some lucky investments along the way, Cindy and I had built a liquid portfolio worth over $100,000. Money grows fast when you start young and don't spend much!

It was time to take control of my own life. I was an expert at creating dining experiences for upscale customers. Also, as a result of my club, and executive dining room jobs, I had great community connections. A friend of mine ran a great "WF" (weddings and funerals) catering business and offered to let me help him at some gigs. I was like a sponge—I observed and absorbed everything about his operation.

Running my own upscale catering business means many weeks of long hours and sporadic income. The executives that I have called on have been very receptive. I guess a good reputation pays off—one heavy-set executive (who apparently loved everyone's food) wanted to "finance" me! I told him that I was self-funded but that he could help by giving me referral business. I gave him some free samplers whenever I was near his office and he always reciprocated by sending more business my way!

Cindy's PR background was also very helpful. She designed some cheap but elegant brochures with the help of a local quick-copy shop. I dropped off them off at the offices of all my contacts. I left a hand-written note and tasty muffin arrange-ments with the their executive assistants. Food always opens doors! I always knew the name of the executives I was trying to reach, and sometimes I used the "He needs this delivery before his 3:00 tee time" routine to get upstairs. My experience in a corporate headquarters and the club did provide some helpful insights!

My "WF" friend contracts the use of a commercial baker's ovens and food storage space. He will subcontract these facilities to me because it appears that we can coordinate the food production cycles and schedules. I don't want to invest in an expensive preparation/storage space at this point in my start-up. My vendor management skills and just-in-time ordering and delivery seem to do the trick for now.

Cindy's mom watches the kids so Cindy can help with preparation, serving, and on-site customer relations. The clients just love her and I do too! Her nieces, nephews, and cousins (she has a HUGE family) help serve our corporate gigs. They are all nice teenagers who do great with minimal training.

I am not surprised at the robust interest in my services. Executives have money to spend and always want things done my way—first class. By using me as a vendor who works outside of their normal in-house, executive food budget, they can turn me loose at high-level client entertainment events. We have had some really cool food events for their high-level clients and these kinds of gigs are very profitable!

I have competition, but I also have my reputation, existing key-person relationships, and no fear of selling and posturing myself as the best. I have come a long way since my days at the burger places!

Bon Appetit!

Web Sites That Were Helpful To Mike:

www.personalchef.com
American Personal Chef Institute—Chef referrals

www.nace.net
National Association of Catering Executives

www.ifsea.org
International Food Service Executives Association

www.entrepreneur.com
PREMEIR business start-up magazine

4

Discover Your Hidden Assets

Renee Reinvents Her Career

As promised, I am finally getting a summary of my journal to you. I struggled after the layoff, but it all came together. Here's my story:

I enjoyed almost every moment of my career in the insurance industry. My friends think I am odd for saying that—especially after twenty-four years in the field. My college internship was followed by my first job as an assistant claims auditor, and from "Day One," I liked the feeling of helping customers.

One thing I didn't feel good about though, was my recent lay-off. Ninety other employees were cut that same day, but how could this happen to ME? You would think that they would appreciate what I have done for them! After hundreds of policy/procedure reviews, budget meetings, training meetings, studies, and morale building activities, I've saved that company fifty times my salary! And I could do that because I became a subject-matter expert over all those years. My most recent boss was in diapers when I started working for the company. And, he often took credit for my work!

I did love my staff though. Dozens of them stood by me when the axe fell. A couple even threatened to quit if I was let go! My past morale building efforts apparently paid off, but I reminded each of them that our small city had few jobs that paid what they earned.

Now what? There appeared to be few jobs in town that paid what I had to earn. And insurance was all I had ever done and all I know. My time at the company had been good to me financially. Even small annual percentage raises added up nicely when there were twenty-four of them! I made more than my husband Bill and his income alone couldn't cover our family's needs. People told me to sell health insurance but I knew that I wouldn't be any good at that.

I had few interviews in our town of 52,000 people. Finding a well-paying job was tough since my whole career to date had been spent in the regional processing office of our national insurance company. There were few other "national level" corporations in town--just branch offices and franchises. There was a possibility at the bank's corporate office, and the money was in my former "ballpark." They eventually hired another person who was about my age "because she had several years of banking experience." I learned to avoid taking rejection personally. A wise friend told me that this is just about my career marketability—not me as a person. **Just because "my" market stinks doesn't mean I am a bad person!**

While searching for the meaning to the phrase "hidden job market," I read a book written by a career coach. The phrase simply means "word of mouth" hiring. Since I have a big mouth, and since I hadn't gotten anywhere with online and newspaper ads, I implemented this immediately.

I made a list of everyone I knew within fifty miles. It listed where they worked and what they did. I started asking everyone listed about possible jobs at their employers. Many had heard about my layoff and were happy to help brainstorm. People really are willing to help if you ask nicely. This action uncovered six leads, two interviews, and one offer I turned down due to the low salary. At least I was being active, which felt good. That book told me to "increase my rejections" which made sense. In my purse, I carried three diskettes containing different versions of my resume. They were color-coded by disk and I gave away a total of five. Their presence reminded me to be networking constantly.

This reminder worked during my regular office visit with Dr. Smith. We were discussing my ongoing medication so I grabbed my prescription bottle from my purse. When I did this I saw those resume diskettes, and told Dr. Smith about my search. We joked about that being a cause of my high blood pressure. But she had an idea and asked me to call her late on Wednesday. Dr. Smith was a shareholder and partner at her large medical practice. She had just been to the practice's business meeting where it was announced that reimbursement administrator had just resigned.

After a week and a half, I interviewed for the position, due to Dr. Smith's introduction. It was not a perfect fit, but I know much about reimbursement and provider-relations due to my former career. My insurance background was finally an asset because they offered me a job, at a slight pay increase over my old job!

After three months on the job, I just love it. The work environment is more dynamic than my previous employer. There was always a new problem to solve and it is all exciting and new to me. I supervise three assistants who make me look good. They say they like me more than my predecessor and our group is upbeat, capable, and fun. It is a nice departure from the more bureaucratic "corporate America." Our culture is based on helping patients and I love doing that!

Working that "hidden job market" paid off for me, and Dr. Smith helped heal my career ailments!

Web Sites That Were Helpful To Renee:

www.ahima.org
American Health Information Management Association

www.naccp.org
National Association of Claims Processing Professionals

www.hcfa.gov
Federal government's Health Care Financing Administration

5

Look For Local Opportunities

Controller Kevin Coddles Start-Ups

My best friend Kevin returned to our hometown after being gone for many years. Career-wise, he was a medium fish in a bigger sea when he worked in Dallas. He earned a Vice President/Controller job with a high-profile high-tech firm. He worked very hard in that job—I know because it would take him weeks to answer emails from me. Even emails about fishing! He regularly moaned about the long hours, lack of structure, and the shifting politics at his company. But, it was an exciting ride and he was smart enough to enjoy the experience and its big bucks.

His employer announced a layoff of 2,000 workers. It would happen over twelve month and Kevin was part of the cuts. I was surprised because in our town of 40,000 people, things don't work like that. Everything is fairly stable and steady around here. Nothing much changes other than the city keeps on creeping our way. It was recently announced that a "technology park" would be built on the edge of town. When Kevin asked me if I knew of any jobs around here, I smiled because I thought he had outgrown us. Unemployment can affect ones' eagerness though, and he convinced me that he wanted to move back home and do the semi-retirement deal.

Laid Off & Loving It!

A guy I knew through the Lions Club was retiring from his job at the city's biggest manufacturing plant. The job wasn't a high profile one like Kevin had, but our cost of living is low and our lifestyle is good. Since Kevin's kids are now out of the home, he could get by on a lower income. Kevin was always conservative, so he could probably handle this type of transition if he got the job. He applied and got the job because he convinced the facility manger that he wanted to come home and help out a smaller company. He was relocated back here in time for our thirtieth high school reunion.

Kevin wanted that job for ten years until he could do early retirement in his late 50's. He happily worked and contributed much to that plant for over two years. His superior understanding of business, finance, and modern processes and procedures saved them significant money. He was a hero to all who understood his work and he loved the pace because he now only worked 40 hours per week.

In March, the corporate office sold the plant and the new buyer planned to move its function to Mexico. There was a loud outcry in the community since about 150 jobs would be lost. Kevin was dismayed since he felt "settled" until the news broke. So, here he was in our small city and unemployed again. He could live for several years on his savings and investments but he wanted to save those nest eggs for retirement.

For weeks he tried to land a job in the area that would pay even two-thirds of what he made before. The economy was tight, jobs were sparse, and nobody wanted to hire a high-paid, "fifty-ish" guy from a "big shot" Dallas firm. The expression, "You can't come home again" must have seemed true to Kevin.

While networking with people during his job hunt, Kevin met professional level people who were in various phases of doing start-up ventures. Some had real solid ideas, some were trying to land financing and a couple actually had some start-up money in hand. What Kevin noticed, he told me, was that most of them were clueless about business growth from the cash flow and financial planning standpoints. He had seen all of this before in Dallas.

Kevin had structured independent contractor and consultant deals many times, and he realized that these maverick start-ups needed his expertise. None of them could afford him on a full-time basis however. Self-promotion was not Kevin's forte but through community involvement, he had run into at least six companies that needed this kind of help. These firms became interested in "renting" Kevin's expertise since he had "name-brand" technology company experience. Kevin structured varying deals with them. He had ongoing retainers and numerous short-term gigs. Kevin billed by the hour, or project basis and his prices were similar to the local CPAs.

Word of Kevin's services spread and he moved from his home office into a small space just off Main Street. He laughed when he told me that one *year's* rent on this office was less than one *month's* rent for a similar space in Dallas. He gained short and long-term clients regularly. His membership in Optimists, Kiwanis, Rotary, and Lions, SCORE and Toastmasters served as his marketing vehicles. Someone at those meetings always introduced him to a prospect and that got the ball rolling.

Eventually, Kevin was turning away business. He avoided hiring employees other than a part-time assistant. People encouraged him to expand but he loved finally being in control of his hours, earnings, and destiny. It is good to finally be able to go fishing with my friend Kevin.

Web sites helpful to Kevin:
www.SCORE.org
Service Corps of Retired Executives

www.rotary.org
International/Local service organization

www.optimists.org
International/Local service organization

31

6

Discover Your Hidden Assets

VP Val Adds Vertical Value

Val was laid off from her VP of Information Technology position at a large hospitality services company. The slower economy was blamed, but Val also suspected possible gender issues too. She was out of the job that she held for eight years. She had worked in computer-related positions in her hometown for the past twenty-one years, and she earned her BS and MS at a local university. At a recent technical conference, she realized how the local IT community felt like a large, extended family.

The severance package for Val included six months of salary plus paid health insurance for that long—the same package offered to all the others who were laid off with her. That money, plus her personal savings allowed Val a twelve-month cushion to find a new position. But she and her husband, who had a good job, wanted to avoid tapping into their ambitious, early-retirement funds. The best scenario would be to get Val back in the saddle with another six-figure job as soon as possible. Relocation was not an option.

Landing that level of a job was a challenge. There were dozens of large firms in Val's city but she learned after several meetings with her peers, that there was very little officer-level job movement. Most jobs available appeared to be two steps lower than Val's former position. The net, outsourcing, co-location, offshore IT projects, too many baby boomer managers, and prolific numbers of consultants, all seemed to work against Val's goals.

An emerging trend Val noticed during her job hunt, was how companies were reducing their IT vendor lists. Cutting the number of product and service providers was a priority of many firms as negotiating with and paying many suppliers had proved inefficient. All IT shops worked with dozens of disparate vendors who provide raised floors, computer cables, computer hardware, software, operating systems, storage, staffing services for temporary and permanent talent, wireless and wired networks, telecommunications services, IT training, and more. There were at least a dozen firms in each product or service category that were trying to gain market share. IT management spent the time managing vendor relationships because purchasing departments usually deferred these technical purchases back to their in-house IT management team.

A friend at a smaller IT shop told Val about their recent capital equipment purchase. Val was surprised to hear the large price difference between that purchase and her former employer's cost for the same product. That fact, plus the news that her replacement at the hospitality firm was already drowning in vendor relations issues, convinced Val of what her next "job" should be. She realized that two of her key assets were vendor management skills and widespread IT community relationships.

Due to rampant industry involvement, local schooling, and high visibility in prestigious, former employers, Val had current relationships with key people at virtually all the major IT shops in town. She contacted her friends and peers at two-dozen leading IT shops, and offered to reduce or remove their burdens of vendor management.

A few shops had a dedicated IT purchaser, but most didn't. Several companies were happy to have an informed, trusted, outside party collect and examine their major technology purchase bids. Director-level and above executives were comfortable to have Val's high level of skill and independent perspective assisting them in this way. They made all final decisions but it was nice for them to have the front-end work handled.

The simple ability to defer dozens of vendor voicemails and emails to Val was, by itself a very valuable service. She gathered her client's requirements and needs and usually fine-tuned what they *thought* they needed. Then she did the initial vendor research and collected the best set of bids, quotes, and prices. Her clients' final decisions often reflected Val's recommendations. Some firms paid Val by the hour, some paid her for the procurement "project," and others paid her a small percentage of the perceived savings she gained through her procurement efforts.

Except for one client that has Val on an ongoing retainer, none of her assignments last longer than many weeks. Therefore, Val learned that she needed to pump out a dozen "marketing" emails a day to her personal network. These emails were personalized and included customized, helpful advice, so she wasted nobody's time. And, she ended up staying as busy as she wanted to be. Not all firms hired her, but she managed to keep busy on a steady basis. She gently yet consistently kept in touch with about sixty local decision influencers and decision makers.

At the end of her first year, Val did not earn her former six-figure compensation. But she did earn three job offers (all rejected by her, due to the salary level offered). She now enjoys more satisfaction, more risk, less hours, higher visibility, and much more fun than she did in any of her years as an employee. And her retirement funds are safe. Her workflow is now fairly predictable and her fourteen "main" clients keep her busy most of the time.

Vendors include her in their sales pitches, because they view Val as a well-connected person who can influence local IT community purchases. Val loves her high visibility role except she now has a new problem: She doesn't know what to do with all of the vendor-stamped coolers, shirts, jackets, umbrellas, pens, mouse pads and sales trinkets that flow into her life.

Web Sites That Were Helpful To Val

www.napm.org
National Association of Purchasing Management

www.pamc.ca
Purchasing Management Association of Canada

www.karrass.com
Negotiation training company

7

Follow the Path of Least Resistance

President Perry Sells Insider Knowledge

Fred,

After our brief chat at our 40th high school reunion, I realized that you were struggling with some early retirement issues. Perhaps my story will be of assistance to you as you make your final decisions. This is a long email, but it may be helpful to you.

I had been President at the company for twelve years. The board originally brought me in to repair their many production, distribution, and sales problems. I knew then that accepting that job was risky, but after a lot of work we became profitable and we assumed a leadership role in our durable medical products niche. My previous experience as a Fortune 1000, Senior VP in this niche prepared me for the role.

It has been a lot of work. I made early, painful human resource actions and that helped clean up some old messes. This was key to our turnaround efforts. My work hours were longer than I wanted, so I missed too much of my kids' formative years. Mary saved the day because all three of our kids have turned out great. Our youngest is now graduating from college, and our oldest is ready to have our THIRD grandbaby!

The company had turned the corner and I was a hero in the eyes of our board. Profits and operations were chugging along smoothly and I ended up getting a little bored. I wanted to retire with this company though, so I hung around a little longer. But when I hit my 60th birthday, I decided to quit and become "Super Grandpa."

We saw a bit more of the grandkids. They were so busy we had to go to their home near Atlanta. Our multi-day visits proved to be hard on my daughter's family and their hectic lives. Therefore, we did less of that than we had hoped we would. After six months of traveling and golfing, and minimal grandkid visits, I was very bored. I guess that you can't retire from being a "Type A" personality, so I was already looking for new worlds to conquer. Numerous charitable causes wanted to soak up my time but my heart is in business.

My former employer's South East operation was having trouble. When I asked around, I learned that the turnover at their distribution facility was rampant. I had fixed these types of problems many times in the past, so I approached the new president with a solution. I had gotten to know him during his transition into his new job, and he was happy to hear my ideas.

I explained my goal was to be partially active on the business front and to be close to my grandkids without being a pest. I assured him that I was staging no comeback, and I only wanted a temporary, low responsibility assignment in that location. The contract I prepared for him limited my assignment to Atlanta,and I offered to never set foot in the corporate home office. Because the South East facility was a bottleneck to the whole company, and since he knew I was sincere, he bought me.

In exchange for long-term residential hotel lodging and a great hourly bill rate, I was to manage the facility for up to six months of the year, on a thirty-hour per week basis. When a perm-anent executive was found, trained, and up to speed, my engagement would end. No additional assignments would be expected or sought by me.

It has worked out great! After five months of this, we are spending the perfect amount of time with the grandkids. My daughter and her husband got to go on a couple of their own trips while we watched the kids. That full-time childcare is much harder than running a company! The firm's operations here are looking much better, I'm making some great "mad money," having fun, and I enjoy free Atlanta lodging!

The bottom line is that I recommend semi-retirement over real retirement. And, your employer is the best place to do that kind of work. They know you and you know them and since they have dozens of locations, I bet you can find some function or location in which to apply your skills part-time. You'll probably get some cheap or free travel perks out of the deal, and work in some visits to your grandkids. I do and I love being "Super Grandpa!"

Best wishes to you on your decisions, and let me know if I can help.

Regards,

Perry

Web Sites Helpful to Perry:

www.nase.org
National Association for the Self-Employed

www.residenceinn.com
International long-term rental suites

www.6figurejobs.com
Executive positions posting site

8

Explore New Ways To Serve

Sandy Sells Her Firm, Now Sells Advice

After a technical and sales career, Sandy started her software company eight years ago. She grew it to twenty-four employees and eventually wanted to implement a new strategic direction. But her angel investors and advisory board disagreed with her vision. After a few employees sold their shares to the firm's backers, Sandy was suddenly a minority shareholder. After one more year of conflict and a slowdown of sales, Sandy conceded and agreed to be bought out. Her $4 Million separation package was fair, based on the firm's sales volume. She was just pleased to be out of the company that had turned on her. To get her payout though, she had to sign a three-year, non-compete agreement that prevented her from working in the software niche she knew best.

After some "R and R" Sandy researched her next conquest but couldn't come up with an industry, business, or niche that felt right. She golfed and lunched once a week at her country club in town but she never felt overly comfortable there due to a lack of other professional women members. One day, she overheard a male member talking about her, saying that the company she built was just a "streak of luck."

That made Sandy angry. She knew firsthand what was involved in starting a business and building it. She knew firsthand how it felt to have control wrested away. She knew firsthand the challenges of being a female business owner. And still people talked like that! The comment inspired her next occupational step.

Sandy dedicated $250,000 of her cash to create an enterprise that empowers women to start, grow, and perhaps sell their own successful businesses. Yes, there were several government programs and non-profit associations with a similar focus, but few were actually run by people with Sandy's level of front-line business experience. Some of these "women's programs" were headed up by men! She networked and researched extensively.

Sandy business became an organization that was in fact helpful to people, but from its inception, it was a "for profit" entity. She didn't plan to be an angel investor unless she stumbled upon a real "diamond in the rough." Instead her focus was to sell information, inspiration, introductions, and mentoring services to ambitious women.

Her distribution model was to conduct low-cost seminars on this topic in regional cities. In addition, her temporary con- tractors sold media units designed by Sandy (books, tapes, CDs, and e-books). Sandy's favorite outcome from these small seminars was landing individual clients who paid modest con- sulting rates for coaching and mentoring. This type of information saved her clients months of time and helped them to avoid spending thousands of "mistake" dollars. Sandy was excellent about introducing her clients to other successful leaders and everyone benefited.

Sandy didn't need the money she earned from this enterprise. And that is why she ended up with a total of 42 coaching clients after her first full year in this venture. Her 18 seminars per year are big drawers and they bring her a fresh mentoring clientele.

She loves helping other women to succeed and grow their ventures.

Web Sites That Were Helpful To Sandy:

www.clientresourcesinc.com
Information Technology Consultancy

www.nawbo.org
National Association of Women Business Owners

www.fwe.org
The Forum for Women Entrepreneurs

www.att.com/wib/
AT&T's Women in Business network

www.t-i-a.com
The International Alliance   Women's' business group

www.thewen.com
Women's Entrepreneurial Network

www.witi.com
Women In Technology International

www.entrepreneur.com
PREMEIR business start-up magazine

9

Market Your Inside Knowledge

VP Bruce Becomes A Business Analyst

Dear Editorial Staff,

Here is the story of how I "stumbled" into the IT business. Please let me know if it would be of interest for your magazine.

Thanks,

Bruce

Being VP of Sales for the Southwest Region for a large office equipment company was great until the day that I was "encouraged" to take a buyout. My years of service and my age added up to more than 55, so I would earn $4,000 a month until my pension plan kicked in at age 62. Also included was one year of my very sizeable base salary. I was in no hurry to take "early retirement" since I was only 52 years young, but, they pushed me through the door by implying that I should take this deal or risk being downsized without any separation package in the future. I really believe that firms today pay people nicely as they kick them out because that makes it tough us former employees to sue!

They didn't care that I had raised profits in all of my regions. This was about the CEO's son getting groomed for the top spot. They figured that my position would get him ready for the CEO job since "Junior" had little sales background. My attorney agreed that I had a good case, but he helped me realize that my former employer had deeper "legal pockets" than I did.

At my age, the job market was brutal. I gathered many leads, lots of interest, but no hard offers. Finally after six months, I used a career coach to help me because I feared that I looked like damaged goods and had just six months of severance remaining. I didn't want to "get by" on that mini-retirement check. The career coach helped me to understand that I wanted to start a part-time business that didn't risk much capital.

That realization allowed me to be open to lower-level jobs since I could supplement that salary with my new side business income. Several employers became interested in me after I lowered my salary demands significantly. I landed a sales manager job in non-competing industry. The comp package was about half of my old deal but it was nice to restart the paycheck routine. I needed to bring home more than that however, so a profitable side venture was important.

My former employer was struggling to implement an Internet, e-commerce sales function. They had too many leaders and not enough experts. The legacy IT staff was stumped somewhat by e-commerce simply because they had few in-house business liaisons. In my opinion, an effective e-commerce strategy is dependant on being customer focused—not IT focused. Help the buyer get what they want simply, elegantly, and cheaply, and they will beat a path to your door. Nobody there realized that philosophy.

I had kept in touch with several execs at the firm. After hearing about this problem, I convinced a couple of them that my inside knowledge plus my new "outsider" status would allow me to be the perfect outsourced solution for this project. I didn't posture myself as the as a computer guru--just as a business/sales analyst who knew their operation and could integrate the needed talent. The IT managers already knew and trusted me.

I got the bid because of the reputation and relationships I had in place. But this was not just a normal bid. The deal was made based on "my staff" delivering this solution on a contingency basis. They would pay me at the end of "Phase One" IF they liked it. Then they'd engage me for the rest of the project. Plus, the work had to be done off site. They wanted to try this plan before paying out multi-million dollar fees to highbrow consulting firms.

I hired an independent e-commerce guru-level consultant who I knew from church. He was to work part-time, which was OK with him since he had other clients he served. He knew the owner of a co-location computing facility too. That company was eager to work with him and me because they wanted to get in the door with my former employer. They allowed us to do Phase One on contingency too. Hey, I am a deal-making VP of Sales you know! My guru put some skin in the game too, by agreeing to work at half of his high hourly rate through Phase One. Ongoing business was important to him too. We were all in this together!

My guru received all of my after-hours time and energy. He knew most of what our client needed but learned the rest of their processes, needs, and operations via a fine-tuned ability to ask sales-oriented questions. I grew in my technical understanding but I avoided the nuts-and-bolts of software development.

Heavy email with the IT department and just occasional daytime phone call enabled us to make good progress on our prototype. The IT manager liked our progress after two months and admitted that his staff couldn't have pulled it off. My many years of sales work in the front trenches for this company was the real reason for my team's success.

The VP signed off on the project's first milestones! In three months, Phase One would go live. When that happens, I will have a nice profit because I bid my subcontractors and vendors correctly. Because of that, we will all win because all my partners will increase their exposure with this client. And we will all get paid!

Phase One is just the beginning. Phase Two will require some intense effort so I will then need to decide if I go back to work for my former employer as a Senior Business Analyst. They already offered this. The pay would be significantly less than my old package but I could keep my seniority and vacation allowance while enjoying a lot less business travel.

I could go another way too, though. I am applying what I have learned in my side business to my new day job. They are thrilled and my career is growing here even though I started low. I will have to consider their promotions also. Plus, I like these people—there is no negative history with them.

Either way, I recognized that my knowledge is power when applied correctly. After six months of struggle, I love having choices and being in demand again. None of this would have happened if hadn't been forced to reinvent myself!

Web Sites That Helped Bruce:

www.guru.com
Broker of Independent Contractors/Consultants

www.pmi.org
Project Management Institute

www.ipma.org.uk
Association of Project Managers (UK)

10

Go With Your Passion

Golf Nut Ned Swings Into a Niche

Golf is my life! Kathy and I are "empty-nest" parents and she is very busy with her work and social calendar. Therefore, golf occupies much of my life. At least that is what my former employer said when they laid me off last Christmas. My work had saved them millions of dollars through my strategic purchasing skills, but in the end, that didn't matter. Officially, I was laid off but it felt like a termination because they mentioned that I snuck out (after my work was done) to the club too often. My job at that mid-sized manufacturing company was really a bore, though!

I got no severance package but we were OK financially. My youngest is headed to college after her military service, so Uncle Sam will help fund her education. Through solid discipline, we have already paid for the house. Kathy's income covers our basic monthly bills but would allow no room for extra travel or our early retirement to an Arizona golf community.

I learned that age and/or wage discrimination is widespread. I look a bit older than my fifty-six years and that doesn't help.

More importantly, the bottom line is that my high wage after thirty-four years of work is the biggest barrier to getting reemployed. I later learned that several of the positions I went for were filled with **younger, cheaper** employees! The job-hunting game was no fun.

During a day of online job hunting, I looked at my collection of golf related magazines, books, toys, videotapes, trophies, software, and décor. Then it hit me. I know and love golf—it is my passion and, it is the growing passion of millions of people, including thousands of people who have plenty of discretionary income. Right there I decided to become a "golf broker."

From my years of purchasing experience, I have become an expert at acquisition. My new business specializes in bringing superior golf equipment and experiences to people who can afford the best. There are over six million "golf-related" listings on the net as one browses that subject. Time-strapped, well-heeled buyers need me to sort through that for them.

Using my manufacturer-relations skills, I contacted over two hundred vendors of golf equipment, software, clinics, travel, workshops, memberships, and events. I offered to contract with them to promote their products and services to my elite clientele for a percentage of their profit. Many already operated using manufacturer's representative models, so as long as they had no territory issues, they were often eager to have an informed, savvy, rep promoting them on a commission-only basis. Some of my "lines" prevented me from calling on retailers or pro shops yet some encouraged it. My purchasing background helped me survive this vendor maze.

The most enjoyable part of this game was my "research." This included clinics, camps, retreats, and clubs that occasionally sent me through their experiences or test labs so that I would know what I was representing. I became a pseudo golf travel agent who was invited to attend some very exclusive golf-related experiences that I would have never been able to afford otherwise. Now I "represent" these entities!

It took me six months to line up most of the corporate relationships and contracts with these product and service providers. During those six months, we did dip into our savings in order to fund the legal, promotional, contractual and vendor-related travel expense. Kathy was behind me on this.

My oldest daughter Anne, who is an information technology graduate, put together an elegant web site for me. It is basically a portal of links to my products and services. It is linked to hundreds of other golf-related sites and it has been key to my success. I got a merchant account at my local bank and my daughter has me registered with several search engines too. I don't know how she does it, but she sure drives the traffic my way. She is one smart kid!

In addition to Ann's web work, I often mention my service to the managers, C-level people, friends, neighbors, and others in my personal network. I gently keep the word-of-mouth thing going. I prime that pump with "special offers" outlined on professional looking business cards. My personal network now accounts for well over half of my business.

One other key to my success is that I network with the thousands of manufacturing reps and salespeople who have tried to sell me something over the years. I kept all of their business cards. Now, I prime that pump via personalized emails. I encourage these folks to send referrals my way. I am sure that I am successful because I continue to prime this pump on a steady basis. As soon as I ignore my personal and professional network of customers, it will dry up and ignore me.

Profit margins vary widely on my products and services. The range is one percent to nearly fifty percent—it just depends on the line and the contract I have in place. My only inventory is the free samples provided to me by my vendors, so my earnings are nearly pure, pre-tax profit. I continue to office at home and my printing expense, travel costs, and Internet expenses are real but manageable. I don't care for the sixty-to-ninety-day wait to get paid by my vendors after a sale. Now I know how all of those vendors who sold me stuff felt about my slow paying clients!

My customer's buying patterns can be sporadic and seasonal. When "Joe the CEO" buys thousands of dollars' worth of equipment, he is set for quite some time. Unless of course I can convince him that he needs to try out that new equipment at an exclusive clinic! A fun deal I have in the works involves TEN senior executives at a former employer of mine who are considering going through me to attend a three-day golf adventure event. A former PGA pro hosts this clinic and my commission for that deal would be nearly four thousand dollars!

Cash flow is up and down but I predict that my second full year at this will see me net more than my old salary level. My goals are being realized because I am having fun and I have not had to dip into our nest egg for living expenses. I couldn't ask for a better way to earn a living because my work revolves around a sport I love, and I get to help other people to increase their enjoyment of the game. I wish I had been laid off sooner!

Fore!

Web Sites That Were Helpful to Ned:

www.shawguides.com
Directory of golf camps for all ages

www.pga.com
Golf schools, equipment, events

www.napm.org
National Association of Purchasing Management

www.the-dma.org
Direct Marketing Association   Marketing trade association

11

Listen To Your Inner Voice

Musical Mary Goes Non-Profit

Dearest Janet,

Merry Christmas to you! I hope your family is doing well. I can't wait to hear from you. Much has happened to me in the last year!

Last March, I was laid off from the job where I worked for nine years. The gas pipeline company was reorganizing and my accounting functions were shifted from our regional office down to corporate in Texas. Because they didn't have position for me in Texas, they gave me a nice severance package.

Job-hunting at age 48 is not a fun thing. I don't think that I am "eccentric" but I got some funny looks during each of my seven interviews. My appearance and demeanor are normal—I just was never a "dress for success" type. I am an individual and went on these interviews dressed as my normal, stylish and unique self. It may have been my appearance, or my age, or my salary expectations, but apparently I don't fit into the new corporate America, as I collected no offers. Odd, since I have twenty-five years of experience. It is sad that there is so much

50

emphasis today on "fitting in" rather than an applicant's actual skills.

Fortunately I had enough severance to keep searching for several months. The time off work also allowed me to pursue my true passion of music. I was never good enough to make the cut as a symphony performer but I am still a wannabe. I love being deeply immersed in and around it—just like when we were in college!

To fill in time while I searched for jobs, I started volunteering at the symphony offices. They were in the midst of a big membership drive and promotional campaign so they welcomed more hands to assist with stapling, mailing, phones, etc. A friend agreed that this would be a good way for me do some new networking. She had told me that I needed to get out and do more mixing in professional settings.

The symphony office had lost one of its key administrators so they were deeply backlogged. My volunteering expanded to twenty-five hours a week. I noticed that the software package they used for one of their systems was outdated and inefficient. I suggested a simple upgrade to the president, and he agreed. My upgrade went in smoothly and there was an obvious improvement to the cash management and member donation systems. They appreciated my idea so much that they threw a surprise lunch for me as a thank you. The Music Director even dropped by for dessert!

Weeks passed and I had no interview activity because I had upped my volunteering to thirty hours a week. The membership and fundraising drive wrapped up and we all thrilled to see that it broke all previous records. We grew by 17%! The president praised the office staff for our efficient handling of the campaign. Due to the new levels of revenue, the board allowed the president to create a full-time, paid position for me!

The financial part of the offer was much lower than my previous pay. And, the assistant-level work was not thrilling to me either. Yet, I realized in the last few months I had felt more alive than at any time during all of my previous employment! I knew that with some adjustments, I could get by on the salary they were offering. I had already cut back on shopping, lunches out, and gift giving, so it wasn't a big stretch to make those changes. I took the job five months ago and I love it!

In my new position, I have contact with the symphony's board of directors. These are mostly high-powered businessmen and women in the community. Two of them have praised my work and told me to be in touch with them at their companies when I finish my time with the symphony! I don't see that happening any time soon though. I love going to work each day. I am so "into" this job that occasionally I drag out my old cello at home and play along with the recordings of the classics. I always close the window blinds though!

Stop by the symphony office when you can. I will give you the tour. It would be fun to get together!

Love,
Mary

Web Sites That Were Helpful to Mary

www.classicalmusic.about.com/cs/orchestras/index.htm
Resource listing of classical music groups

www.artswire.org/current/jobs/html
National job site for arts-related jobs

www.vcmfa.org/volunteer
Sample of volunteer opportunities in the fine arts

12

Remember Your Marketable Skills

Tool Man Tom Helps Others

The family's small, Midwestern hog farm didn't generate enough income. His mother's job in town helped hold things together for them. As a result of growing up in that situation, Tom and his brother learned how to fix everything that broke. Their equipment was less than modern and the boys and their father were the best repair guys around. Sometimes their farm repair jobs literally relied upon duct tape and bailing wire.

After high school, Tom joined the military to get away. In the Marines, he tested very high in mechanical aptitudes so he was assigned to several shops during his time in the service. He flourished, but returned to his Midwestern roots after a very positive four-year stint.

He returned to his hometown but not the farm. My grandfather eagerly hired Tom to work in the one-person machine shop. Grandpa's 62 years made it hard for him to do the heavy physical work required. They repaired farm equipment and created custom tools for a few small plants around the area. Tom worked with Grandpa by day and took night courses over at the technical community college.

Tom was smart as a whip and incredibly innovative with his head and hands. Grandpa said Tom did the work of two men. Grandpa's customers all heard about Tom's high capability. Even though I was just seven at the time, I remember Grandpa bragging about Tom to the guys at the coffee shop. I wanted to be just like Tom when I grew up!

The shop hired a couple of part-time, after-school teenagers to help Tom out. Those extra hands helped grow the business during the time that farm prices forced farmers to hang on to their equipment longer. The coffee shop men teased Grandpa when he announced that he was buying fancier tools and expanding the size of the shop. Tom became a 20% partner after his first year.

Tom graduated from the community college's tool-and-die program and went on to increase the "plant side" of the shop. He visited area manufacturing plants, studied their needs and usually came up with a low-cost, homegrown solution that enhanced their production. Tom impressed more than one "educated" engineer.

After two more years, seventy percent of the business came from the tool making side of the business. Tom's clients came to rely on him to create specialized machines or tools that assisted with their production needs. Retooling was a regular process for these small manufacturing companies because their product lines kept changing.

Grandpa wanted to quit his "PR" role at the shop and sell Tom the business. But Tom had no lump sum and a marginal credit rating. They worked out a deal where Tom paid Grandpa for the shop over a twelve-year period. The selling price accounted the new business Tom had brought in. Everyone was happy.

Tom had married started a family. I went on to be an aircraft mechanic for a major airline. Tom grew Grandpa's shop over the years, becoming a full-blown, tool and die shop with specialized equipment and clients all over the region. After 25 years, Tom wanted to sell out, retire, and see the "world" via an RV. I bought the shop and its eight, highly skilled employees. History repeated itself as Tom sold me the shop and agreed to owner financing. He remembered me being the kid who hung around his grandpa's shop so he cut me a good price.

Tom and his wife Brenda took most of year off and they traveled extensively. Their kids were out of the house and he and Brenda traveled to 42 states and Caribbean. But after that, Tom was itching to get busy so I invited him to a trade conference in Kansas City. THAT "got his juices flowing" again!

At that conference, I introduced him to people who used to sell equipment to my shop at the airline. Those people knew a lot about who was doing what in the field. Based on my introductions, Tom's reputation, and his likeability, several of my contacts went on to introduce him to even more key players. He gathered up many business cards and brochures about new technology and issues in the sector.

Tom was like a kid in a candy shop and I knew he would never last as early retiree. He chatted with several vendors there and left with some contract projects in mind. He determined that he was going to be a "consultant to industry." That sounded funny to him but it meant that he got to make and design stuff again. He excitedly told me about some of the pending projects as we drove home.

I helped Tom structure a small business aimed at delivering his intellectual property and skills. Clients would bring him in for an outside opinion or to add innovative, creative insight into their equipment-related production problems. He kindly referred new business to my shop and in return I encouraged him to use our facilities. He relished his new role, recognition, and project oriented income.

Tom loves his new schedule as he has time to enjoy fishing, camping, and traveling but he still feels connected to his passion. He often turns down projects, referring many of them to our capable staff. He stays just as busy as he wants to be and he always has a bench to tinker around at my shop. Grandpa would be proud of us both!

Web Sites That Were Helpful to Tom:

www.allianceofconsultants.com
Directory of diverse consultants

www.amtda.org
American Machine Tool Distributors Association

www.metalforming.com
Precision Metalforming Association (PMA)

13

Listen For Hidden Opportunities

Fast-Track Frank Goes Financial

When I started at the IT consulting company, we were just a handful of sharp people with good ideas, vision, and great timing. In just eight years, Mike's company bootstrapped its way to a company with branch offices in eight principal Southeastern cities. Our company's revenues approached $30 Million and life was very hectic but fun.

As employee number four with the company, I prospered. I was named as national sales manger and all client relationships ultimately reported to me. I was *the* top rainmaker and earned just over $300,000 in compensation during the best years.

Then we hit some obstacles. The demand for IT staff augmentation services was slowing, project work replaced some IT contractors, national players had noticed our success and had moved into our markets, the first wave of "e-business" had come and gone, and clients were sending some projects to offshore. Plus, there was a lot of talent available that our clients hired directly. We had earned our revenues based on a shortage of IT talent and skills but that issue seemed to be slowing.

Our attempts to reinvent ourselves did not work—we weren't able to turn the corner on becoming an "e-business consultancy." Revenues slipped and Mike grew restless. I had spent all of my energy on building my compensation package at the company. It never occurred to me to focus on stock and ownership. Therefore, I only had a token amount of the private stock. I thought Mike would own the firm forever, but I was dead wrong. One day, he announced that he had signed a letter of intent to sell the company. I couldn't breathe!

My personal overhead was high so I was in a risky situation. The buyer of our company was a bigger player in the industry complete with their own national sales manager. After four months of new ownership, they let me go with a severance package of six months of base and commission income. That package plus the sale of my small stock holdings in the company would get me through most of a year financially. But then what?

I interviewed with several companies that discussed offering me less responsibility and less money. It is true that the only time you control your destiny is when you control your own business. Mike was fat and happy and I couldn't find a job that paid half of my former peak earnings. And I needed to be concerned about keeping my creditors "at the lifestyle to which they had become accustomed." I had nearly one thousand personal business contacts in our West Coast city, but not one of them converted into an appealing job offer.

While meeting with my financial services representative on 401K issues, I went on to chat with him about his work. Mark had always impressed me with his professionalism and expertise. When he heard that my job search was not going well, he encouraged me to consider joining his company. I had always viewed myself as a business-to-business sales person. I did not know much about doing business-to-consumer sales. But when you have no job, you listen to all leads.

Depending upon the ability of the sales rep, Mark's firm had a couple people who actually exceeded my former peak income.

Yes, they had been in their industry for a long time, but despite that I felt like I had finally found a national, "brand-name" company that was interested in seeing me earn a LARGE income.

I passed their interviews, and weeks later, I aced the tests required to sell investments and insurance. Selling both lines of products/services allowed me to make just about anyone into my customer. This was nice because now EVERYONE was a lead—not just people in the information technology niche.

Cool features in the financial services sector are the renewals and asset trailers that contribute to a person's income. In IT contracting, we had ongoing revenue (and commissions) for the life of the project only. In the insurance business, I get renewal commissions for long periods of time and I know how to *keep* customers happy over the long haul. This supplemental source of ongoing income is nice.

On the securities side, I chose to provide services on managed-fee basis so I can focus on the "big-picture" of my clients' needs. My one thousand contacts were key to my fairly quick start in this business. My ramp-up *did* take many months, but I am a great salesman who is unafraid to professionally approach anyone. Now I help many people achieve their personal financial goals.

Two years after joining this industry, I have paid my dues and I am starting a focus on serving the securities and insurance portfolios of high-net-worth clients. Even Mike is my client now! I love the process of building the wealth of my clients.

I work a few less hours than I did at the consulting company and now have three financial analysts reporting to me. I am building an exciting future and feel that I have a ton of control and independence, yet a peer group and national structure behind me. I definitely see myself as a *national* sales manager and leader with this company. I arrived at this point after hitting a huge speed bump, but it looks like smooth sailing from here!

Web Sites That Were Helpful to Frank:

www.newyorklife.com
Premier financial services company

www.luthbro.com
Lutheran Brotherhood--Premier financial services company

www.ml.com
Merrill Lynch--Premier financial services company

www.naifa.org
National Association of Insurance and Financial Advisors

www.brokernetusa.com
Full service insurance agency services bureau

www.test-n-learn.com
Training Company preparing people for securities licensure

14

Helping Other Helps You

Bored Bob Joins Boards

July:

After all those years with the firm, I wanted to slow down. I reached the level of Assistant VP of Finance at our Fortune 1000 conglomerate, and I couldn't believe that it was thirty-two years ago that I started as a Staff Accountant Trainee. My boss, the CFO encouraged me to take the nice separation packages that were being offered. He and I had worked together for many years and he suggested that I worked too hard.

My age and years of service combined to make me eligible for an early pension that more than covers our living expenses. The house, cars, and kids' educations are all paid up so I did decided to "cash-out." I want to supplement that pension income, though. That will allow some world-class travel and let us help our kids get started in their new homes. I'm not willing to touch our nest egg for those costs.

Starting or buying a business isn't interesting to me. I worked for a big company and I don't want to play around with a little one. Even absentee ownership is more than I want right now, and consulting equals too much running around for my tastes. I have done my share of corporate travel.

October:

Our trips to Rio and Greece were fantastic. The tour companies spoiled us rotten and I loved reconnecting with Joyce, my bride of 36 years. The trips were great but it sure is quiet around the house. Joyce has a full social calendar so it is just the dog and I hanging around.

I was asked by a friend at church to serve as board member for a prominent non-profit organization. Joel knew I was recently retired and a bit bored. The timing was perfect and it is an honor to be asked to join this group. Executives in town typically seek out this type of appointment, due to its high visibility. We meet once a month but there is committee work, so I will be getting together with folks more often than that.

November:

This charity does a great job serving its clientele, but they sure need some financial controls! Other folks on this board know how to help, but they don't have the time needed to fix things. Nor is it their job to do so. I have the time and the ability to help, so I plan to offer my services. I estimate that it will only take around a hundred hours to make some real improvements.

January:

Tom, another board member at this charity, is a CEO of a 2,500-person corporation in town. We have come to know each other through the charity. He asked me to serve on his corporate Board of Directors. He liked what I have been doing for our charitable group and he went on to say that he just had a board seat open up and my finance skills would be helpful to him. I agreed to join him and was thrilled to later learn that this assignment paid an annual stipend of several thousand dollars, plus a tad of company stock and some travel perks.

March:

While serving on Tom's board of directors, I realized that this "career" was a perfect fit for me. I have no daily commitment, no employees, few politics, lots of status, and even an occasional corporate trip. And, the skills I picked up over nearly forty years in finance allow me to make some solid board level contributions. It is so enjoyable that I want to do more of this.

November:

My "portfolio" of board of director seats has grown to four. Plus, I still serve on two non-profit boards. My network has grown and I am now invited to more of these types of assignments than I chose to accept. My personal network of business contacts, church, and Rotary contacts have proved to be "too" successful. My reputation and personality must help. I turn them down now because I don't want to be too busy.

My non-profit boards do good work. It is fulfilling when we make the world a better place through our big-picture ideas and execution. My medium-sized, public and private corporate board assignments are surprisingly generous. Trips, meetings, stipends, stock, and cash make me feel like a "rock star of corporate finance." I am just as busy as I want to be, Joyce and I are having fun, and my golf handicap isn't getting any worse. Life is good!

Web Sites That Were Helpful to Bob:

www.mapnp.org
Board/Management assistance to nonprofits

www.bbbsa.org
Youth mentoring organization

www.girlsinc.org
National youth (girls) organization

www.bsa.scouting.org
National educational program for boys

15

Rearrange Your Thinking

VP Patrick Goes Up The River

September:

I can't "retire," I'm only 41 years old! Someone out there must need a seasoned, marketing VP! But I think that I am getting automatically rejected when I discuss compensation! But I am worth that money because I grew top-line revenues by 26% for the two lines of our sports equipment division that I headed up. Nobody knows distribution, manufacturing, and marketing to retail better than me! Am I really too expensive?

With Jan and John in private school, and their mom working just part time, we NEED a lot of cash. Throw in our "mini-mansion," our foolish hobbies, and we will be in trouble without the salary that I am used to.

November:

My interviews in and outside of the sporting goods industry have produced no hits. One prospect was an emerging technology firm owned by a guy at the country club. Everything was cool until they came in with a "sub-$100K offer." I made that 6 years ago!

December:

Looking back, I should have seriously considered that tech company offer because things have really been slow. It must be the holidays. I need to land something soon because my severance dries up just 6 months from now. Ginger is back to work full time and she hates it. The kids are coping but they don't like my crabbiness. Well, I don't like their teenage crabbiness either.

Perhaps I will sort things out over our traditional Christmas road trip back home. Ginger loves the small town, "up North" Christmas charm. I love it too--it was a great place to grow up. As kids, we loved our water sports and hunting and fishing activities. Those experiences most likely helped me to passionately sell sporting goods equipment later in life!

An hour from my folks place, we stopped for gas next door to a canoe rental/outfitter company. Its "For Sale By Owner" sign prompted me to chat with the guy who was shoveling snow out front. Lyle and his wife Ellen were selling the business after twenty-one years. They could no longer handle the physical demands of the enterprise. He told me he was asking $295,000 and he thought I should buy it! HA!! We continued on and had a great holiday at my folks' place.

January:

I returned home to a few reject letters from the twenty-seven resumes I sent out in December. A new trend in help wanted advertising appears to be a line that reads: "Only the most qualified will get a response." It should read: "We are too lazy and too busy to treat you like a human." Sometimes I think job-hunting on the web is just a handy way to increase the volume of rejections.

After some fruitless Internet job surfing one day, I just picked up the phone and called Lyle. He remembered me from our brief meeting and we chatted for over an hour. I now have all the financials for this small business. His price includes the company's vans, trailers, canoes, canoe equipment plus the old home and storage building on almost 8 acres of wooded land. I played with the numbers all night. Using my severance, our investments, 401Ks, home equity, credit-worthiness, this deal looked possible! Lyle and Ellen owned everything outright and he offered to do some owner financing. In his best year, Lyle's business netted less than half of my former income. But we do have a high "suburban overhead."

February:

Ginger is seeking counseling about my unemployment. That makes **me** crazy because I am the one who needs help! I have one offer that is coming soon—at about 2/3 of what I used to make and it involves relocation to a more expensive city. Not too bright to do that move. I don't have time to rise up through the ranks again. I can't get that canoe business out of my head but how could I ever convince Ginger and the kids?

March 2:

Tonight I made the sales pitch to my family to buy the canoe rental business and move up North. I used my best corporate presentation skills. I included benefits, risk factors, cash flow diagrams, and more. This Power Point presentation far exceeded my best-ever corporate dog-and-pony show. The kids did not want to leave their friends. I anticipated this objection and offered that we might be able to hire their pals for summer help. I also pointed out that they would meet many other kids their age in this tourist hotspot. John missed the cut on the football team last year, so a fresh start in a smaller school appealed to him. Jan seems to be stuck on the wrong path socially right now so she thought that this could be a way to start over.

Ginger was very quiet. This would mean living in a small house, working a million hours a week all summer, leaving her clubs, friends, and church. She always knew that the future might require a corporate move, but this? But, her father died last summer so that helped her clarify some of her values. Being a "corporate wife for life" was not her life's mission.

By the end of the week, everyone was coming up with a new idea about how we could improve the canoe excursion business! Ginger's main idea, however, involved moving our present home to that river. They were coming around! Unbelievable!

Mid March

Lyle got my offer today via fax. It is contingent upon selling our house, which has appreciated very nicely over our nine years here. It should sell quickly—I heard our realtor salivating during my call to her. That home equity, some cashed-out investments, and Lyle and Ellen's private financing will make this a doable deal!

Late March

The deal is DONE! I feel ALIVE! Way Cool!! Our house is closing next month so the paperwork will then be complete. I am headed "Up North" to learn everything from Lyle and Ellen. I can already think of fifty ways to improve "our" business—I AM a top marketing executive, you know!

August:

We have never worked so hard! Everyone in the family is too busy to worry about adjusting to this new life. Due to the small house and teamwork nature of this venture, I am getting closer to kids than I have been in years. Ginger and I are feeling closer than ever too. My only corporate travel now is to haul canoes one way or the other along the river. We have rediscovered what we liked about each other. Plus, we have both lost weight, and got a tan so our romantic life is better than ever—even though we are often tired! I think Ginger is so happy because she feels like she feels needed again. And boy, is she needed!

Jan, our Webmaster, can make that computer sing. Her skills and my marketing background have provided us effective, low-budget promotions so we already have some solid leads on reservations for next year. Lyle and Ellen bought a little house in town and they come visit often. He is amazed at our "marketing muscle." Business is steady and retail impulse buying is high. John occasionally hosts an off road bicycle tour (we have a few bikes for rent) and he is getting in great shape for football.

Former sporting goods industry contacts have agreed to give new equipment discounts and even "donations" to our small business. They gain "real world" focus group feedback from testing their new stuff through our business because I write strategic marketing analyses about customer response to their products. And we are building up our sporting goods retail component too.

During the off-season, I will dust off my carpentry skills and add some more retail space. We hope to try cyber-retailing out of our front office where customers handle equipment in our building and purchase a similar item over an Internet kiosk in our store. They are more likely to buy while they are in the wilderness, and it will be drop-shipped to their homes. We'll get sales commissions on those sales but carry almost no inventory! I am a genius!

If trends continue, we will finish out the first season with a net profit somewhere near half of my old income. That represents all four of our "salaries" combined! We've never worked this many hours but it is fun because we are doing this venture as a family. We used to all be headed separate directions so this is much better! We put in long hours together and help our customers really enjoy themselves. We add some personality to it to so they experience memorable experiences. It is fun to help others have fun and we are good at it!

Web Sites That Were Helpful to Patrick:

www.nasgwa.org
National Association of Sporting Goods Wholesalers

www.sginews.com
Sporting Goods Intelligence – Industry statistics

www.amrivers.org
American Rivers – National river preservation group

www.canoecountry.com
Minnesota Boundary Waters area information "portal"

www.ustoa.com
United States Tour Operator professional association

16

Do What You Do Best

Radio Ronnie--The Show Must Go On!

It has been a fun career. I have been performing since high school and I studied broadcasting at college. Then my radio career got started and I was in the right place at the right time. I love radio--the talk, the music, the format strategies, the on-site promotions, etc. I loved being a "regional talent" for my music/call-in show. At my peak, we were even getting considered for national radio syndication of my show. I earned our station lots of money off my show's expensive commercial airtime. Just when syndication talks were starting though, my format dropped cold dead. The fan base for a show like man literally disappeared almost overnight. I was a "has-been" in my twenties!

Because I was in good standing at the station, they offered me the program manager position as long as I sold airtime on a "part-time" basis. At first, I was appalled to be asked to sell ads. After all, I was "talent." But since I had spent most of the "big money" I earned when I was a hot, I had to consider all options.

My "semi-fame" helped when I sold ads. This was somewhat due to the fact that the station had put my face on lots of billboards when my show was hot. I did a lot of self-training and eventually excelled and became sales manager. Of course corporate noticed this and I eventually became regional sales manager over 12 stations. The money was good and the responsibility felt right. A steady job was good since Marie and I had now been blessed with two children.

Life moved along like this for many years until consolidation raised its ugly head. Our radio station holding company merged with another similar company. There was not room for my regional level position so I was cut. "Change" and radio go hand-in-hand so nothing surprised me anymore. But I did need a new source of healthy income. Marie stayed home with our kids so she brought in no income. Fortunately our debt load was low and I did collect three months worth of severance pay.

Repeating my on-air success again was improbable. My old show was a fluke of the times and couldn't be duplicated. I checked out real estate, insurance, executive recruiting, manufacturer's rep, retail, and corporate sales manager jobs. None of them particularly grabbed me.

While driving home from a final interview for a sales position with an office equipment company, I noticed the sign for a DJ service. I had never really noticed that sign before. Of course I knew that those firms were out there but I had never thought much about them because I was a broadcast personality—not a "trunk of a car wedding reception personality." I visited that company's web site when I got home. It was an intriguing business.

I received an offer from the office equipment outfit, but knew I didn't want to spend the rest of my occupational life figuring out profit margins on photocopy machines. I talked to Marie who was very supportive, and we studied the mobile entertainment industry extensively. After a few weeks of intense research and planning, we decided to take the leap and try our hand at using my former "celebrity" to become a *Mobile Entertainment Vendor*.

We borrowed some money from Marie's dad for the venture. We didn't know half of what we needed to know to actually succeed in this venture but our heart was in it. We began acquiring equipment, music, leads and "bruises."

There were many pitfalls along the way. Cash flow, travel and set-up difficulties, constant night work, music inventory issues, and rotten crowds, were a few of the obstacles. Despite those difficulties, I loved what I was doing because I was making people happy again. I earned a few bookings due to my former "fame" because some folks actually remembered my show. They were eager to book me because I was a throwback to a time when they were more carefree.

Money was tight until I learned what to do get some daytime events. I finally figured out how to use my former customer base from my radio sales days. I enthusiastically entered the "corporate entertainment market. " Companies have sales, product, training and every other kind of meetings daily. Most hotels in our area hosted some company or association meeting nearly every day.

I obtained the city's visitor and convention center booking information that listed the various meetings that were coming to town in the future. From that data, I used my outgoing personality to approach the contact people in charge of those meetings. This took some investigative work, but it has proved to be a very worthwhile source of gigs for us.

I have convinced several event planners that strategically placed music and light entertainment will enhance their events and I have numerous testimonials that I email to my prospects. Many planners spend thousands of dollars on professional speakers and presenters. Why not hundreds of dollars on music?

For these corporate meeting clients, we do music trivia events, pre and post speaker introductions music, background music for awards, karaoke events, and break time music. These firms loved the extra punch provided by my superior command of the right music for the right time. I built up to doing three business/corporate events a week so I was able to cut back to doing just two weekend events per month. That was a nice from a family perspective. Companies pay better than wedding parties. The meeting planners are mostly interested in quality issues when it comes to these high profile events. And not one corporate music gig goes by without me getting at least one viable wedding lead!

This business still requires heavy "roadie" work. The setting up and tearing down of my music library and equipment does get tedious at times. Emerging technology though is lightening that load some. Even with my ergonomically customized dolly, there is a lot of lifting as we prepare for and exit from the shows. I hired Marie's eighteen-year-old nephew to do part-time roadie support. He is a good, entertaining kid who would probably do this work for free just to be around this business. He has a band and doesn't want to go to college yet. His back has helped to save mine!

I love being a "Musical Master of Ceremonies" and my business now grosses over six figures per year. Marie runs the books and the scheduling from our modern home office. We all work hard, but we enjoy making people's lives more interesting and enjoyable through music and entertainment. It took a lot of effort to get to the point where I can say this, but I wish I had been laid off sooner!!

Web Sites That Were Helpful to Ronnie:

www.skylord.com
Referral listing of radio job boards/links

www.nab.org
National Association Broadcasters

www.mpi.web.org
Meeting Planners International --Convention planners group

www.adja.org
American Disc Jockey Association—trade group

17

See The Value of Your Assets

Sales Rep Rick Rents His Database

As per your request, here is a "journal" of how I got started in my new endeavor. Use it as you see fit and I hope my story helps someone else out there.

Thanks for your encouragement during my career transition. By the way, interest in what I am doing is very strong. I already have NINE "vendor partner" proposals in the pipeline! I love this concept!

Thanks again,

Rick

February 20th

The merger of the two biggest companies in my product sector will probably kill my sales rep career. After 23 years of being an independent manufacturer's representative in the medical equipment sector, I now fear a huge income cut. My three most profitable lines are being taken away. Worse than that, I can't pick up similar lines through other companies because our acquiring firm has bought out most of the competition. They "bought" nearly all the market share! And they use employee sales reps on a base salary and low commissions. They will probably want to hire me but that would mean cutting my income by about two thirds.

I put in over 35,000 miles of windshield time last year. My territory is over a thousand miles wide so I am always on the go. I do want my high income to continue, but isn't there an easier way to do it? People think it is glamorous to host clients to golf, sports events, lunches, dinners, and such, but it can be a grind after many years. The good news is that these efforts have paid off nicely for me. I have built hundreds and hundreds of key relationships with buyers. But that still needs to be maintained.

I have been self-employed for most of my time in the medical equipment world. I love that part because I like the boss! So, looking for a job with another firm is out. I would be a lousy employee!

March 21:

It is bleak out there! Most viable product lines have been secured by some other rep or company salesperson. It would be possible for me to do sales work outside of the medical equipment sector, but I hate to dump over twenty years' worth of contacts and relationships. Selling just my secondary lines won't cover the price of gas. "Big Brother", the acquiring monopolist doesn't even want to hire me—they hired some "snot nose" rookie who has a whopping *two-year* track record of selling computer equipment!

I have liquid investments that will allow me to pay my household bills for a long time, so I am not too nervous. But I don't *want* to use that money for groceries and house payments. My wife Deb and I are restless because I will soon be receiving my LAST commission check from my former best line. That's a sinking feeling.

April 3:

I visited with a career coach who really helped me clarify my goals, needs, and plans. He helped me realize the career assets that I possess. I knew this already, but a neutral endorsement by an expert really put me on the right track. We discussed that I am a persistent, likeable, dealmaker and he then helped me realize another huge asset of mine: I am a relationship builder with thousands of relationships already in place. He explained that a person's number one asset is often the thing that is "closest to money." So, my strengths, interests, and passions are what will make me the most money and make me the happiest. My deep network of buyers in the medical sector is unmatched. Talking to the career coach was like going to a shrink because he helped me realize things that I did not see.

May 15:

Now things are taking shape. My many buyer relationships manifested over the years are now **"For Rent."** Instead of trying to find some*thing* to sell to these 1,200 plus key buyers, I am going to rent access to these people. My ability to get this group of doctors, nurses, therapists, secretaries, purchasing managers, VPs, hospital administrators, and CEOs to respond to me is a valuable asset. They get hundreds of sales pitches so their attention is worth much to other sales people.

Hundreds of companies want to sell products and services to **"my"** buyers, so I will introduce other sales professionals to them—for a fee. I will promote my "introductory services" at every medical conference, association meeting, and vendor show that I can get into. I will charge a flat fee, a steady retainer for my time, or, earn a percentage of the profit made from the sales I broker. I will get my clients (sellers) in front of my historic buyers.

Only the vendors who I respect and trust will be able to become my clients. My reputation means everything. In effect, I will act as an outsourced purchasing service. I won't do the final purchases, but my former buyers will rely on me because they trust me to save them a lot of time by screening out bad deals. Only the best will be my clients and be introduced through me.

Some sellers may not be thrilled to give me a cut of what they earn through my contacts, but the smart ones will realize that 90% of the proceeds off a sale is better than 100% of the "proceeds" from NO sale. We all know that it takes up to six months to crack open a new account. I can drop that to six DAYS for my clients!

My niece, the public relations professional, is nearly done with my simple but elegant brochure and basic web site that explains my service.

August 18:

Demand is high! The word in my niche is out and I have several manufacturers interested in becoming my clients. I won't be able to handle them all. I will need to stick to a limited number of clients so I can maintain high quality on my "filtering" efforts. I need to cut back on my promotion of these services or charge more because *too many* sellers have approached me to perform this service for them. I have become a "manufacturer's rep's rep!"

I have **nine** vendor deals that are being hammered out or finalized right now. I think this concept has tremendous financial potential and it looks like I will have a lot less windshield time. My selling clients will do the presentations and follow-ups so I don't have to be present much. If demand for this service stays strong, I may even make some money teaching other reps in other territories how to do this! I am having fun capitalizing on my assets!

Web Sites That Were Helpful to Rick:

www.medmatrix.com
Pre-owned medical equipment brokers

www.sdms.org
Society of Diagnostic Medical Sonograph Imaging

www.aha.org American Hospital Association

18

Promote Yourself

VP Leon Hypes Himself

July:

Did you hear about Leon? He is one of those who are getting the axe! You would think the many legislative issues affecting our health insurance industry would require us to hold on to an influential PR/Lobbyist like him. He is one of the best in the state. I heard he has solid relationships with all the key state legislators. I heard that our firm now plans to hire contract lobbyists to represent us to the state legislature.

My friend Sam is also being released during this layoff. He has been here for eight years--just like Leon. I don't know how they selected the 36 people that got cut, but I am glad that I wasn't one of them! But, any one of us could have been chopped.

I wonder what Leon is going to do--he is a VP and he makes big money and ours is a tight job market. He is a lawyer by training, but I heard he didn't want to practice in a firm. I guess he enjoys lobbyist settings more than private practice or general counsel work. Leon's son is a starter on the high school basketball team so I bet they don't want to relocate.

June:

Did you hear about Leon? He has a whole new career! My friend Susan from Finance lunched with him the other day and here's the scoop: Leon is now a professional speaker and consultant! His severance package was lame, so he didn't have a any money to get his business started. After having little luck landing another corporate job, he postured himself as a short-term, independent consultant to companies. People were interested in him on a temporary, independent basis and he molded that into a consulting and speaker business.

It seems that our competitors, vendors, customers, and others are interested in hearing Leon's expertise and opinions about our industry. He earns up to $4,000+ PER DAY for a speaking or consulting gig at companies and association meetings. And it sounds like he has several engagements a month! My friend Susan said that Leon's success is due to his tireless self-promotion and self-marketing.

The funny thing is that Leon never seemed to be a "sales type" of person. But he WAS always pitching and persuading others to do things that were good for our firm. He did work the "human network" like nobody's business—he was ALWAYS on the phone or emailing people. He probably made dozens of outside contacts every day as he worked to shape public opinion of our firm. Sounds like he is still hustling like that.

Susan said that Leon works the same network of people that he built when he worked here. She said that he has a compelling pitch that is unique to him and captivating to his potential clients. He postures himself so potential customers think that they are **missing key information if they don't hire him!** I saw his promotion package and his web site. He really looks like an expert—and a lot of that knowledge was gained while he worked here!

It sounds like a great life. It appears that people can have great money, travel, prestige, independence, recognition, and stimulating work if they promote themselves as hard as Leon does. It tires me out think about how hard works. I see his promotions everywhere--in the industry rags, newsletters, and at every association or trade meeting. Leon offered to buy me lunch next month to get my opinion on a key industry issue. He wants MY opinion so I will be happy to tell him what I know.

I have to get to my meeting, but it's fun to hear about Leon's success, isn't it? I will let you know what I learn after I meet with him!

Web Sites That Were Helpful to Leon:

www.igab.org
International Association of Speakers Bureaus

www.walters-intl.com
Speakers bureau and speaker training firm

www.naspeaker.org
National Trade Association for professional speakers

www.lobbyistdirectory.com
National Lobbyist Directory & Guidelines

19

Who Do You Know?

Mainframe Mary Moves Within

Her layoff wasn't particularly shocking. Each year Mary's financial services employer routinely let go about two hundred of their 4,000 person corporate office staff. There appeared to be an unwritten rule to purge a random five percent of the staff before the annual stockholder meeting. Employees referred to the regular event as "Black Thursday."

Mary had been with the company for over ten years. She was a computer operations supervisor over a very specialized, small group that coordinated the Job Control Language functions of the IBM mainframes. It was a customer billing system. At some companies, software developers do this work, but Mary's company had allowed an evolution of this function to become its own little department. She managed seven full-time staff and had worked her income up to a very respectable level. On this Black Thursday, her employer purged her whole group. Mary's severance package was generous—about a month of pay for every year she worked there.

The job market was harsh. She had landed her previous position with the firm as a hands-on data entry person after testing high on an aptitude test at the Workforce Development Office.

84

Prior to that, she held clerical jobs. Her natural ability enabled her to move up nicely during her time with her employer. Due to the specialized nature of her work though, it was hard for Mary to get considered at other firms. Few firms even had this job role and the ones that did had virtually no turnover.

Mary worked on her job hunt for over six hours each day. Her resume was professionally prepared, her attire perfect, her attitude tops, and her drive strong. But she could not land an interview—despite several versions of her resume. She started leaving the 'salary history' and 'salary expectations' boxes blank on applications, and that got her more interview action, but she still couldn't get hired. By Easter, Mary was very discouraged, as she had sent out 89 online or hardcopy resumes. This had led to five interviews and only one final interview—all with NO job offers.

Mary was ready to accept a customer service position at an insurance company that paid forty-percent less than her former job. Her severance fund was fading fast and her family relied upon her income. They bought their nice home just three years ago based on the perceived stability of her job. Because they could not make ends meet on her husband Jerry's income alone, she had to land another job.

Before accepting that job, it occurred to Mary that there were similar positions at her old company. In fact, there was a whole department of people doing this kind of work. And Mary knew Jane, the supervisor of that area because they were both on the com-pany's softball league. She put the insurance offer on hold and called Jane for lunch.

Mary realized that her former employer was still conducting its day-to-day business. They hadn't crumbled without her and corporate life there was chugging along. Mary's separation file said she was eligible for rehire, but her pride and anger had blocked her from even thinking about going back to work there, until now.

Jane and Mary quickly updated each other over pasta. There was an assistant supervisor position coming available in the Customer Call-Back Department that reported to a friend of Jane's. Mary's background was perfect—technical skills, high attention to detail, supervisory experience, strong company knowledge, and a super personality. Jane spoke to her friend Michelle who granted Mary an interview.

Of concern to Michelle, was the job's lower pay grade than what Mary held in her old IT job. Mary assured Michelle that months of unemployment made any job with the company look great. She assured her potential new boss that she would not attempt to get other internal jobs for at least 18 months. Mary's former supervisors provided stellar references and Michelle liked Mary's determination to prove herself in a new area. Mary was offered the job at a 25% pay cut from her old job. Mary viewed this as a 75% increase over her "present" income of ZERO!

Mary started back with the firm and was a quick study. She kicked herself for taking so long to job hunt with the people she already knew. The new department was more fun than her old job and Mary's family cut some of its spending and is doing just fine. The added perk is that Mary's previous vacation time and retirement accruals were reinstated since she was gone for just six months.

At any new employer, Mary would have only earned two weeks of paid vacation per year. Since she was able to reclaim her five weeks of vacation, the pay cut figured out to be not quite as severe. The new salary was an adjustment, but it seemed easier cope with now. Mary is happy and her family is too. And she is very actively working on making herself "irreplaceable" at work.

Web Sites That Were Helpful to Mary:

www.dol.gov
Federal Department of Labor

www.doleta.gov
DOL's Employment, Training & Displaced worker program

www.acinet.org
America's Career Infonet—DOL statistics & services

www.ajb.org
Americas Job Bank—DOL listing of jobs and talent

20

Follow Your Heart

"Mr. Auto" Loves Cars

John,

I met this crazy guy the other day at a swap meet. He has a cool story so I bought him a beer, knowing that your magazine is always looking for unique auto-related stories. Here is the story he told me about himself and his career. He is known as "Mr. Auto" but his real name is Larry.

Larry's dad was a mechanic who loved cars. Larry's best memories of his dad were the times when they spent endless hours of tinkering on various vehicles. Larry grew up to become "Mr. Auto" because he could tell you make, model, and engine sizes of almost every American car made since the nineteen thirties. He said he has bought, sold, owned, traded, and parted out over 100 cars in his lifetime.

Larry spent hours on the net and with car magazines at public libraries and bookstores. His dad told Larry to go into a field other than mechanic work as a profession because Larry could always work on cars as a hobby. Since he hung out at the library so often, he determined that the "white collar" job of working there would please his father and still allow Larry to be close to automotive information. Library Science was an unusual college major for a guy with grease under fingernails, but he said it was a good way to meet women.

One woman he met in college was Jackie. They fell in love and got married after their graduation. Larry landed a part-time, librarian job at a smaller county library. That arrangement worked well since he could work on friends' cars at their homes after his short workweek. They paid him for his time with cash or some barter item. He eventually moved into a full-time job at a suburban Chicago area library. The commute was long but the job represented a good opportunity.

In the next several years, he and Jackie had a daughter. Larry kept working on cars and researching them too. He built his reputation as a connected guy who could find and appraise models and parts. He could swap, barter, and introduce buyers and sellers in several automotive genres during his off hours.

Larry wished he could quit his library job and pursue the passion that gave him so much recognition. His job however, provided the insurance benefits for the family. Jackie made excellent, money working part-time for a high-rolling real estate professional, but there was no insurance coverage with that job.

An election year rolled around and the incumbent mayor cut the library budget. Years of library budget growth had turned the library system into a campaign issue. Larry was the last full-timer hired at his branch so he was the first to get let go and he did get a sixty-day notice. He was a popular librarian due the steady stream of automotive seminars, and speakers that he regularly lined up. Several car clubs were now meeting at Larry's library branch meeting room.

The couple's daughter was now in school, and Jackie went to work full time for a major transportation corporation. She joined the logistics department and worked in an administrative capacity. She became the benefits provider for the family but Larry still had to also recreate his former income. He had offers to go to work in auto parts stores, sell autos, and even be an auto mechanic, but Larry wanted to build his automotive information empire.

He focused on locating and the procurement of hard to find parts or vehicles for buyers and sellers. He cut a deal with those buyers and sellers where he would earn a finder's fee when he enabled a transaction. His research skills allowed him to be very effective at tracking down the people and things he needed. Since he never actually owned any of the parts or vehicles, he did not need a dealer's license, but he did form an official business entity.

Over the years, he developed a database of over 1,000 automotive-related contacts, and due his library science background, he had organized it very strategically. He could instantly access and find vehicles, parts, vendors, suppliers, and people with his computerized database. His finder's fee income grew but was still up and down. Certain deals were very lucrative but often there were no deals at all. At those times, Larry had a somewhat steady stream of restoration work on people's hot rods and classic cars. Many car buffs that Larry knew didn't have time themselves to get their cars ready for shows and contests. They would often hire Larry to help due to his positive reputation.

Larry then created what turned into six subscription newsletters. Each one catered to a tight niche within the automotive genre. One went out monthly but the others were quarterly. It was time consuming but fun and Larry found that he had more energy with this business of his own than he ever had while working at the library. Also, Larry developed hilarious automotive-related talks that he gave at auto shows and swap meets. He sometimes gets paid a few bucks for these "appearances" but the real perk is the exposure he earns for his newsletters. "People like to 'relate' to the person behind the data" he said.

Laid Off & Loving It!

While at the library in the mid 1990's, Larry realized that the Internet was going to become big. He obtained his own domain name and built a makeshift web site with the help of some computer-oriented car buffs he knew. Larry's site promoted his finder's services and his newsletters.

His six specialty newsletters have grown to a have "many" paid subscribers. He wouldn't give me specific numbers. Libraries and auto enthusiast clubs across the country pay for Larry's insightful, helpful and passionate view of their niches. Larry's information serves as a filter to their respective markets. Also, people him pay for advertising space in the "buy/sell" sections of the letters. This is a good profit center. His newsletter niches include hot rod, Corvette, Nomad, Thunderbird, muscle car, and Harley Davidson.

To market to libraries, Larry appealed to the way their buyers think. He convinced these purchasers that he was a former librarian who knows that these newsletters can increase traffic at their libraries. That would help them to justify an increased budget at their branches. A direct-mail post card drained a chunk of the couple's savings but it pointed library buyers to online samples of his literature products. Slowly but surely, he built a library subscriber base. "When you add up all of the college, high school, and public libraries out there, the library market is exciting." Larry said.

Larry has subscribers in several countries and he keeps his letters in hardcopy format. His web site only offers samples of a few past issues. He says that this formula works because his customers are tangible, "hands-on guys." It also helps him keep the relationship feel in his enterprise. And this differentiates him from hundreds of online sites. He is a master, though, of Internet linking. He claims to have his home page linked to over 400 automotive related sites!

Jackie cut her job down to thirty hours a week so she provides the insurance benefits and helps Larry run their enterprise. Larry's sister comes over on a regular basis to offer more hands-

91

on help during mailing weeks. She majors in journalism and loves to work with Larry and Jackie. Larry has taken over the whole basement of his large ranch home to grow his business.

I will get you his contact information because he is very interested in being the subject of an article in your magazine. He would be a good story because he is living his passion and earning some good money at the same time!

Websites That Were Helpful to Larry:

www.ala.org
American Library Association

www.autoscribes.org
Automotive Press Writer's Assn.

www.hotrod.com
Hot Rod Magazine

www.mygokart.com
Classic Car Clubs

www.classicar.com
Classic car community

www.corvetteclubofamerica.com
Corvette club

www.harleyswap.com
Harley Davidson swap site

www.motortrend.com
Comprehensive auto magazine

21

Profit Through Service

Nurse Nancy Serves Many

Thanks for asking about the history of how and why I made my career transition. Here is how it all worked out:

First of all, I love kids. I grew up in a large family and together with my great husband, Alan, we have four of our own. Even in high school, I knew that I wanted to be a pediatric nurse so I pursued that profession with a passion. Upon graduation, I took a job at our city's large children's hospital.

Working there mended and broke my heart each day. I can't describe how useful I feel when I provide comfort and healing to an ill child. But, there is the other side—the patients who we are *only* able to provide love and comfort to.

Over the years, I worked into a part-time role at the hospital. That was helpful since my kids, age 4 through 14, are very busy. Alan's career and pay were moving ahead nicely so my contributions of part-time pay worked out. We are very involved in our kids' church and sports events so it is nice to work part time.

Laid Off & Loving It!

Last winter, the unimaginable happened. Alan was laid off from his high-tech employer. He was not alone--dozens of others got the axe too. His employer was having some financial difficulty so there was no separation or severance package. I immediately went back to full-time work status. **It was tough because of the children's schedules.** Alan's unemployment lasted three months. His skills are in high demand, but the tough economy made his search stretch out.

After Alan's paychecks resumed, I wanted to return to part-time work. Since the hospital was experiencing shortages of staff, they pressured me to not go back to part-time status. That made me wonder if I liked them anymore. The hospital was a forty-five minute commute from our new home. I thought about finding a job at the pediatrician's office that is near our neighborhood. And, I really started thinking about what my occupational calling should be. Someone once wrote, *"When you are ready for a thing, it will appear."* I wondered if that applied to me.

That month, our associate pastor asked me to substitute for a youth group volunteer who had to pull out of an upcoming weekend youth retreat. My 12-year-old was scheduled to go on that trip so I happily agreed. The event included the pastor, six other adults, and forty-five middle school kids! The pastor asked me to lead one of the class sessions. I declined because I was not qualified, but the pastor gently pressed me to try. I did it and received good response from the kids and excellent response from the adults. My many years of volunteer teaching paid off that day because I did well and had fun!

A month after that retreat, the pastor asked me to go lunch with him and the senior pastor. At my favorite Italian restaurant, they explained to me that our church's rapid growth demanded a new level of staffing. The full-time youth and education director was going to focus on youth only, so we needed to add a full time parish education coordinator.

They wanted ME to think and pray about considering that Parish Education Director position. The position would pay for thirty-two hours per week. This would mean a few more hours of work per week, and at less pay than I was used to. The job involved organizing, leading, managing, recruiting for, and teaching some of the many educational ministries at our church.

After intense prayer and talk with my family and friends, I agreed to go through the church's formal interview process. In the end, I was thrilled to be called to the position. There were other, better-trained candidates who applied but I got the job due to the church's comfort level with me. I felt very alive and excited to start this new ministry. The lower pay didn't seem to matter as Alan's new job paid even more than his last one.

I work more than thirty-two hours per week, and my kids are involved in many of the programs I teach or lead. I feel my work is a good example for them. The church is just two miles from home, so I enjoy flexibility with my work and home schedule. The staff is wonderful and the work is very rewarding. Being part of the faith journey for students of all ages is very exciting.

I now enjoy a strong sense of calling, and my family appears to be handling the transition quite well. My youngest now sees me more than ever because I can often bring him along to work. Alan's career interruption and my substitute role on that retreat combined to lead me into this ministry. I was ready for a thing, and it appeared!

Web Sites That Were Helpful To Nancy:

www.nurseweek.com/careers/articles.html
Industry periodical with career advice

www.churchpros.com
Career transition support for church professionals

22

Know and Work Your Niche

Principal Paula Plans Parties

Hi Bob,

Here is the advertising letter you asked me about. I hope it helps you as you consider starting your business. I know this letter works because I am busier now than I was when I was principal of my large middle school!

Some additional comments follow the sample letter.

Best Wishes,

Paula

* * * * *

To: The Event Planner
From: Principal Paula
RE: Your upcoming event

Your retirement sendoff for Principal Adams will, I'm sure, be one of the crowing events of his career. Perhaps my services can make it even more special.

My Name is Paula, and I am the founder of Parties by Paula. We specialize in the flawless execution of parties for unique and special occasions just like yours.

I have come to know Principal Adams through many years of shared professional experience in various city school system events. He and I worked together on a citywide task force a few years ago and during that project, I came to know "Mr. A" as a man who is highly deserving of a terrific retirement sendoff.

Being a long-time educator myself, I offer you the following quiz to those in charge of planning the event:

1. The best reason to consider use of a top meeting and event planner for this event is:

   a. We don't know what the budget will be for the event.

   b. We are all very close to Principal Adams and this event will be very emotional.

   c. All of those who are planning the event are active, busy professionals.

   d. All of the above

2. Which of the following is most true?

    a. A professional event planner has the professional connections to enhance your party's content.

    b. Paula has twenty-five years of experience as a volunteer planner of events of this type.

    c. Paula has two years of experience as a full-time PROFESSIONAL meeting planner for education related events.

    d. All of the above

3. How can *Parties By Paula* save **you** money on this event and still insure a high-quality occasion?

    a. Paula's suppliers and vendors compete with one another so Paula's prices are low.

    b. Many of Paula's suppliers discount for "non-profit" events such as yours.

    c. Paula's meeting incentives and door prizes can drive a higher attendance and therefore volume discounts.

    d. All of the above.

Of course the answer to each of the questions is "All of The Above." My thirty years in education gives me a full understanding of the dynamics involved in your event. Here is one testimonial you might enjoy:

Dear Paula,

I can't express enough gratitude to you for what you did for my retirement party. While your visibility AT the party was basically zero, I felt your presence in every detail. The food was exceptional, the atmosphere exquisite, and the speakers were great.

I have known those speakers for decades, but your direction allowed their presentations to elicit steady laughter and tears. I know this is true because they told me what you did to prepare them for the event.

Anyway, thanks so much for everything. Your event summarized my career nicely and the memories will last a lifetime.

Thanks again,

Superintendent Petersen

In review, the quiz and the testimonial speak for themselves. I would be happy to visit with you regarding some particulars and specifics of an event like this and then give you a quote on costs. Even if you elect not to use my services at that point, I will still provide you with my handout entitled, "Paula's Pointers For Perfect Parties."

Best Regards,

Paula
Parties By Paula

* * * * *

Bob, I appeal to people based on my "insider knowledge" of the educational community. I go after retiring educator events because I know that niche.

I met hundreds of educators over my career in the greater Minneapolis area and staying in touch with people keeps my business very visible. I have "lookouts" that are always keeping their eyes open for me. And my educational niche very often becomes a door opener for the competitive wedding and reunion market.

As I mentioned, I am almost too busy these days. I have done this work full-time ever since my early retirement two years ago. Last year I made more money than I did as a principal! My first year was a financial bust, so I was glad my husband Tom was still employed.

Word of mouth referrals, a tight niche, strong attention to detail, sales ability, and excellent creativity have combined to create my new occupational life of prosperity, purpose, and passion. I should have started this business years ago!

Let's have a cup of coffee soon so we can brainstorm about your potential business start-up.

Sincerely,

Paula

Web Sites That Were Helpful to Paula

www.incl.uncg.edu
Career development site for teachers and educators and others

www.iami.org
International Society of Meeting Planners

www.ka-ching.oxegen.com
Business/entrepreneur media for women

23

Build On Your Strengths

Pastor Pete Motivates Corporate Congregations

Thanks for requesting to hear my story of career transition. Moving from my former career to my present occupation has not been easy, so perhaps my personal tale contains some nuggets that will be of value to this group.

My career transition started five years ago, after 23 years as a parish pastor in a Protestant denomination. My last call was at a multi-staff, medium-sized church in a Pennsylvania community of about 65,000 people. I had been at that church for eight years and we were doing good work. The congregation was comprised of many young families. I worked long hours and we had steady growth and things were sailing along.

One group of very vocal members had emerged, though. They were very adamant about a theological issue and the proposed expansion of our building. Specifically, they disagreed with the amount of debt we should take for new building projects. The short version is that our congregation ended up splitting over this issue. Despite my decades of work as a shepherd and a mediator, I couldn't resolve the philosophical split that had taken over this young church. I ended up being caught in the middle and eventually, without a calling or a job.

My wife Lisa had developed a nice career in the psychology department at the regional medical center. Because she was just then realizing some of her potential there, and because she spent over two decades chasing my career around the region, we chose to not consider another church position in a new location. We loved the community and our home.

But, I needed a job and an income. Lisa's salary alone didn't pay all the bills. The church gave me six months of pay upon my departure as long as I promised to take my church membership somewhere else. Honoring that request was easy!

For years, people told me they loved my sermons and preaching. I was often invited to speak at other congregations and church-wide events. Congregants often asked me for printouts of my sermons. We made audio recordings of our worship services and made them available to all. A local radio station carried our Sunday services and they often stated that my sermons were popular amongst their listeners.

So I had a big head when it came to my presentation ability and I fervently researched the concept of becoming a paid public speaker. For years my ministry had seen how adversity affects people and how different people respond to it. Hundreds of counseling sessions with parishioners have given me a solid background in this area. A recurring theme that I had witnessed was how, with God's help, people can be highly resilient.

Becoming a professional speaker is what I decided to do because I could travel as needed and Lisa could keep her job. I attended two workshops by industry speaker-trainer professionals. I read a dozen books, many articles, and bought several recordings on the topic of paid public speaking and consulting. I built my presentation content into one-hour, half day, or weekend retreat versions. I made demo recordings, built a template-driven web site, and I was ready for paying clients to beat a path to my door. Then a strange thing happened: *Silence.*

What I learned over the next year is that a professional speaker needs a great presence, a good web site, some demo recordings, a timely topic, and superior platforms skills. But, what he needs MOST of all is steady, constant self-promotion. And I had not been doing that.

I was doing steady pulpit supply for vacationing pastors in the region so I had been bringing a little income into the home. But Lisa and I elected to liquidate one of our investments so I could continue to pursue my expensive "hobby." Without Lisa's support and belief, I would now be selling real estate instead of inspiration.

Again, I studied the top pros through the National Speakers Association. I bought more resources, practiced, and watched. At another speakers' workshop, we were discussing the topic of selling our services. Right there I realized that my former career did not involve what is officially called "sales," but I in fact, had *years of experience in persuading people*. I learned that selling is simply telling a persuasive story and then persistently following up. I had been a mission pastor who started two congregations from scratch, so I finally realized that I had been a "salesman" for years! Duh!!

I immediately made a mental transfer of skills and began marketing *myself* (instead of a new church) with a vengeance. I did newsletter articles, talk radio shows, leave-behind bro-chures, hundreds of personal networking telephone calls and emails, sample recordings given to key corporate managers I knew and didn't know. **I even promoted myself through local churches!** My daughter taught me how to make links to dozens of other web sites.

I gave free mini-talks to every group or service club that was within sixty miles of our suburban community. I didn't work on my content much anymore—instead I focused on my self-promotion at least two thirds of the time or more. And it slowly worked! My promotional efforts finally started paying off. I followed my mentors to the letter and ended up being somewhat in demand on the topics of individual change and crisis management. The book about transitions, **Who Moved My Cheese** by Spencer Johnson and Ken Blanchard was popular at the time, so it was nice that my theme piggybacks with theirs.

Being postured as a "business-savvy" clergy person was also an attention-getter with meeting planners and corporate officers. The hot trend had become holistic treatment of employees during turbulent economic times. And that was a Godsend for my business.

I wrote a fifty-page booklet on my theme. It has no fancy binding or cover but I still manage to sell many copies through my "mail me a check" web site and at all of my presentations. When I use real-life stories of people who have suffered and still come out on top, my audiences respond. They sometimes get tearful and communicate their appreciation for my stories. Then they purchase my products!

It took time for me to adjust the fact that I shouldn't just give away my written and recorded products. But, I have come to terms with selling my information though. I believe that if my audiences support me, I am able to continue to afford to be "out there" to support them.

Often, after my speeches, people ask me to follow up with a visit to problem areas at their companies. I don't know much about corporate business, but I do know how to listen to folks, and that is mostly what they need. And they pay me to do that!

The bottom line is that by using all of the tools I just mentioned, I have managed to double my top pastoral income. I earn between one and three thousand dollars for most presentations, sell a respectable amount of recorded and printed products, and even get paid a few dollars for listening at clients' corporate offices. There have been several dry spells, but I stay fairly busy.

This didn't happen overnight—we nearly had to move out of our home during year two of my new career. But, it has been a wonderful second career. Without my first career I would have never been ready to do something like this. I loved that work and I also love this work. And I give thanks to God for the resourcefulness of the human soul.

Web Sites That Were Helpful to Pastor Pete:

www.nsaspeaker.org
National, non-profit speakers association

www.churchpros.com
Consultants to Ministers In Transition

www.pastorsnet.org
Resource lists of clergy transition services

www.amazon.com
Carries "*Who Moved My Cheese*" by Spencer Johnson and Ken Blanchard

24

Simplify Your Vocation

Researcher Rick Burns Up The Slopes

I met a guy who you'd be interested in hearing about. I met him last week while skiing in Aspen. He has a pretty cool life. We were doing the small-talk routine while going up a chair lift. When he told me about his interesting background, I told him that you were working on a book about career transitions. Due to that, he let me learn more about him over lunch. His name is Rick, and he is originally from New York City. He has lived in the Rockies for three years now and he is an "online ski bum."

He grew up in ski country in Vermont and went on to graduate from a prestigious New England college. He immediately landed a job applying his economics and public relations majors. It was an entry-level job in the investor relations department of a huge chemical company based in the New York City area.

He flourished in that department because he liked the action. The public relations department handled the news media most of the time, but Rick knew that the Investor Relations department was the behind-the-scenes group that kept the real investors informed. Those institutional investors and fund managers demanded more exacting data than did the general press. And Rick's department provided that. The C-level execs handled most of the fund managers personally, but a fair amount of routine inquiries were handled by the IR group.

After about a year with the firm, the company suffered a crisis regarding the rumored toxicity of one of its general use products. In the hour that the story broke, a major institutional investor could not reach his normal C-level contact so he called the Investor Relations department. It was lunchtime so nobody was in the department except Rick, who took the call.

Even though he did not have details, Rick was great on his feet and he calmed this institutional pension fund representative. The caller demanded a sophisticated analysis, which Rick did not provide, but he did manage to reassure the investor. A senior official at the fund later told Rick's boss that Rick's real-time feedback allowed them to save face with **their** constituents who were concerned about the chemical firm. Rick didn't single-handedly keep that fund from dumping its holdings, but he certainly helped his employer that day.

He did earn a nice bonus out of the deal and hung on to work in the department for three more years, eventually earning the title of Assistant Manager of the Investor Relations department. That group had low turnover, however, and Rick was ready for advancement. **This made him susceptible to a head-hunter's call that encouraged him to join the dot-com revolution.** In a new position with a dot-com start-up firm, he would be the director of the department and earn thousands of stock options.

Rick scrutinized the backing of the firm. Investor support was plentiful and the business model actually seemed poised to earn a profit. He took the job and adeptly built an excellent investor relations function.

After two years and three rounds of investor financing, the firm was on the edge of profitability. However, one of the key investors died suddenly and the other investors then backed out. Now they looked like so many other e-commerce companies that were in trouble. The only thing that could save the firm was another shot of about $20 Million, and Rick knew that would not occur in the current business climate. Rick and his co-workers were dumped, worthless stock options and all.

Rick went skiing in Colorado to ponder his future. He had been a hero in a huge corporation, and a key man in a crashed start-up. "So what's next?" he asked himself. On the chair lift, he met a self-employed management consultant who detailed the pros and cons of his business to Rick. This man earned a good living and seemed to have a nice sense of control over his life and schedule. Rick decided that this is what he would do for next "career" which was about to begin at the age of 28.

Rick was not a salesman or rainmaker kind of guy so he figured out how to peddle what he knew. He determined that his unique selling proposition was his ability to find, obtain, package, and deliver strategic, investment-related research. He wasn't going to be a broker or a Wall Street analyst type, but sort of a "private detective" of strategic information. If a company want-ed to know some market or competitor trends, they could contract with Rick who could create customized, strategic reports.

He could be used to find information that firms themselves wouldn't or couldn't get. He doesn't do any illicit espionage or illegal, dark stuff. Rather, he is gifted at getting information over the net, from libraries, and chatty, "former" employees. The data he uses to create his reports comes mostly from these sources.

This guy is a master of the Internet. After the lifts closed, he showed me his set-up. He knows how to use public and purchased data bases better than anyone I have ever seen. He IS a private net detective! Rick has "reciprocal agreements" and strategic links with dozens of high-visibility web sites. Some of these high-view link sites have become customers of his so he barters for a link on their site in exchange for free or highly dis-counted research. He gets some of his customers from that.

The other more enjoyable method of marketing is what he did with me—meet people while on the chair lifts. High-level people from all over the world come to Aspen. Rick has mastered the art of small talk that leads to business. He starts by asking where people are from and what kind of work they do there. Then he impresses folks by telling them some obscure fact about their own employer, company, or competitor. This often leads to a request for his laminated business card. He keeps them in an easily accessible pocket. This guy has turned the traditional "elevator speech" into a "chair lift" speech! He says this technique provides him with over 50% of his business. Potential clients meet him in person and are instantly impressed.

The best part of the deal is that he doesn't work much. A custom report may cost his client $500 to $5,000 depending upon its scope and deadline. And those fees last him awhile. His attic (apartment would be too generous a term) is just a bed, a small fridge, a dresser, and his extensive workstation. He re-located out to Aspen with no debt and no family. He works out of this 300 square-foot space. Those net links and chair lift pitches serve as his only advertising so the guy has very little cost. His "pad" cost him only $700 a month because it has no bathroom and was just wasted storage space before he moved in. Rick has an agreement to provide the local health club with demographic customer reports in exchange for discounted food and free use of their shower facilities.

His only business expense is his cable modem, nice letterhead, report packaging materials, postage and his season pass lift ticket. He said he completes about three projects a month, skis everyday, and works at odd times. He never puts in more than 25 hours per week. He grossed about $36,000 last year and often turns down business (especially on "new powder" weeks). He says he can't work too much because he still has to work on his skiing form. This guy loves his life and he was an inspiration to me!

Web Sites That Were Helpful to Rick:

www.aspensnowmass.com
Awesome Rocky Mountain ski resorts

www.niri.org
National Investor Relations Institute--Trade Association

www.donnellymarketing.com
Consumer/business database and information services

www.infousa.com
Database, information, and list services company

25

Enlist the Help of Others

Analytical Amy Makes An Alliance

I hate interviewing for jobs, finding jobs, and even thinking about getting a new job. That's why I was a bit overwhelmed lately with my layoff. Nobody could fault my track record as I only had one sick day in the whole 14 years I was with that media company. Fifty people were let go that day, including me. It will still take me awhile to process this. I don't know how they are going to get by without my contributions!

My field is soft right now. There is a bit more supply of talent than jobs to soak up that talent. I know because I have conducted studies and made reports of the supply and demand for accountants like me. This data is based on several Internet related sources such as the Workforce Development Office, various local and regional job and resume posting boards, and the good old Sunday paper. I don't really want to move but I will if have to—after exhausting all local leads.

I have read the books and studied many web sites on 'how to get a job in this market.' It all comes down to selling and promoting myself which I hate doing. I excel for employers once I am in the door, but I do poorly in my approaches and interviews.

I told my dilemma to Leslie who is our church council president where I head up the finance committee. Leslie works as a VP of Sales for some local software company. He immediately took me under his wing. He fixed my resume and told me to get dozens more of them out on the street. I had been carefully responding to one position at a time so I wouldn't overlap or confuse the job hunt process. And, none of the positions seemed quite right for my background. Leslie told me that if I didn't gather five rejection letters or emails a week that I just wasn't serious about getting a job. Well, I am very serious. I have some reserve savings and investments, but I don't want to use them for groceries.

I followed Leslie's advice, but it seemed that some of that activity was truly pointless. However, I did get two new interviews scheduled, so I guess it wasn't totally pointless. I went on them both, getting a quick rejection from one and getting ignored by the other. Leslie knew people at both of those companies (he knows EVERYONE!) and he later learned that the folks who were hired had similar backgrounds to me.

This led to phase two of our career-marketing project: My presentation. This part was torture for me. He had me over for a family dinner followed by "interview practice." It was like having my teeth pulled at first, but he gently showed me my weaknesses and built up my strengths. I am no rap star yet, but I can now rip loose with some blurbs about my occupational strengths. We even practiced salary negotiation techniques. That man is a brilliant marketer, but dumb as a post with regard to accounting!

My flurry of improved resumes, together with my improved interpersonal confidence helped me get some more job interviews. And, my "portfolio of interview answers and sound bites" helped me earn two good job offers. Those events helped

112

to build my confidence, but I turned down both because they weren't quite right for me.

In the interim, Leslie checked with a guy he knows at a big insurance company. He thought that his friend was always looking for someone like me. Since Leslie knew my skills from the church finance committee, he gave me a high recommendation. I went on that interview and they started talking about an offer. They must have liked my sound bites because they made me an offer! And, Leslie's negotiating tips helped me **earn a slight increase** over their initial offer. I turned their 5% increase (over my former salary level) into a 8% increase! I accepted the job and start next week. It looks like a great fit.

In closing, I simply want to encourage *you* to be honest with yourself while job-hunting. Are you really worth what you think you are worth? If so, why, and how can you prove that? If you are weak in resume writing, interviews, and negotiating, get help from someone **with** strengths in those areas! I found Leslie and it helped a ton. Who is YOUR Leslie?

Web Sites That Helped Ann:

www.aaa.org
American Accounting Association

www.aafa.com
Accounting professions placement company

www.insurance-jobs-center.com
Placement company for insurance professionals

www.creativementors.com
Coaching and mentoring company (United Kingdom)

26

Determine What You Want and Need

CIO Leonard Levels Out

My career represented the American dream. For seven years, I was a Vice President of Information Technology, reaching that post after twenty years of previous experience. And it took just twenty minutes to flush that all down the toilet.

After drifting around in low-wage jobs following my Army stint, I applied for a computer operator job at a large insurance company. I had picked up computer exposure in the Army so I showed some experience, and was apparently moderately hirable. My graveyard shift lasted about a year until I was pro-moted to the evening/swing shift. I nabbed a daytime slot one year after that.

The work was boring but I watched and learned from the other data processing staff. I determined that I would in fact earn more income by going the programmer route, so I enrolled in night school to study for that. I got my associate degree eventually and applied for a programmer trainee position. My good internal work history and my ability to get along with people helped me to land that job.

114

Programmer Trainee through Project Leader was my eventual career track there. I planned and targeted each promotion and earned them in a manner somewhat close to my plan. Internal power struggles and people problems sometimes slowed me down, but I handled that because I was a "student" of internal politics while in the Army.

My progress stalled out after twelve years with the firm, so I took that headhunter's call one day and ended up leaving the company for a job at a large local bank. I had earned a BS degree in night classes and I had started my evening/weekend MBA program. My new function was Senior Project Leader reporting to the Assistant Vice President of Information Technology.

I loved that job because many of the bank's projects and business applications flowed through me. It was hot seat and it was great. After two years and many weekends, I earned my MBA. Four years later, Bob retired from the AVP slot and I got his job. Then, six years later, I was promoted to the VP of IT position after that position became vacant.

The VP of IT job was fun. I liked the status, power, and influence that I had over my department of 300-plus employees. We made many productive changes and improvements and fought the typical battles of an organization that size. Things were going well until my old friend Pete called.

Pete used to be my boss at the insurance company, and he enticed me to join a dot-com start-up company. This firm looked like it would create several millionaires. My current comp package was well over six figures, so I was cautious. But Pete knew that I needed another world to conquer. He was right. I ended up joining the 31-person start-up firm because their business plan was good, financing secured, and their solid management team hired me as an officer. I said yes after they matched my salary and threw in 250,000 stock options.

The short version is that we secured our second round of financing came in and we grew to over one-hundred employees. We started getting some market share, approached profitability, and built good brand recognition in our niche. Then, like so many others, we died in a burning "dot-bomb crash." I was on the street just seven months after I left the bank and I didn't know what hit me. There was no money available for severance packages!

The bank had filled my old job and avoided bringing me back as consultant because of the bad message that would send to the current staff. They had leadership needs but they acted like the conservative bank that they were. I switched my accounts to another bank.

Being in my forties, I was much too young to retire nor could I afford to. My large family had come to rely on my healthy income. I contacted all of my friends and contacts in the industry and they were all supportive but none of them knew of a job for me. The kids were too entrenched in school to even think about relocation, plus our East Coast city is large and progressive—few other cities could offer a better business climate than this one.

After three weeks, I landed an interview with a small banking software company that had a staff totaling forty people. They had a nice ten-year history, a solid base of customers, and steady profitability. I accepted their offer that was a 35% cut from my bank salary, but I "happily" did so because the market was tight and I wanted to get back to work. They appeared to be very stable.

This was "Bad Career Idea Number Two." My "dot-com" experience was an intoxicating ride due to its fast pace and lack of structure. My new firm however, clearly just wanted me on board to be their "poster boy" to the banking industry. After a few weeks it became apparent that they wanted me to just go with their sales reps on sales calls. Also, the very technically oriented owner ran the whole development process himself and wanted little advice from anyone there, including me. Their product was good but they were not ready to move beyond a "mom-and-pop" operation that was run by "Pop." I love to sell and I can be very good at it. Deep down though, I a manager. The gig lasted six, painful months.

I was on the street again and my family was upset. The economy had worsened and jobs were tough to find again, but I applied for an IT manager position at the county government. I was overqualified for the position and the pay package was low. After a two-and-a-half month interview cycle, I received and readily accepted their offer for the job managing a ninety-five person IT department.

After many months on the job, I am starting to implement many plans and actual improvements. There are numerous budget and political realities here. The responsibility is less, the pay is less, the pace is slower, and the budget is tight. But, do you know what? I love it! My glamorous and wild career rides were fun, but this is good work for this point in my life. We have adjusted to the income level and I enjoy the many challenges we have that are found only in this setting. The best part is my 40-hour work week, I haven't had one of those since I was a computer operator. My job is steady and the family seems to enjoy getting to know me again. Life is good!

Web Sites That Were Helpful to Leonard:

www.monster.com
Leading online jobs/resume site

www.ajb.dni/us
Americas Job Bank, DOL's jobs and resume source

www.careersingovernment.com
Online resources for government employment

www.federaljobs.net
The federal government employs nearly 3,000,000 people

27

Never Settle

Ex-Jock Joe Sells Youth Fitness

DAILY TIMES   October 17

Joe Johnson was the starting quarterback on his high school and college teams. He played for an NAIA level college football team that placed second nationally.   During his tenure in assistant and head coaching jobs, his teams secured five all-city championships and one state football championship. Johnson clearly has a tradition of winning which is how he has approached his youth fitness gym. "I make my customers into winners," brags Johnson. After teaching and coaching for nearly twelve years, he shocked his coworkers four years ago by announcing his resignation.   Nobody in the teachers' lounge understood Johnson's vision that day.

Since then, his youth fitness center has taken off. He recently added more square footage to his strip mall location. "Fitness is more important than ever for this generation of kids. They are growing up with video games and computer learning and being very sedentary. We get those kids moving."

Apparently, their baby boomer parents agree. "Two career households that are strapped for time are our main customers." Johnson explains. "Their kids may or may not be in soccer, baseball, and/or dance, but parents enroll with us to assure a balanced fitness regime for their kids."

His center holds classes for children age four through seventeen. His charges get fit through a wide variety of games and activities, both structured and unstructured. "Our rule is that kids have to be moving for the length of their session" says Johnson. "But we have many fun activity centers so that is easy to do."

Trampolines, gymnastic equipment, parachutes, relay courses, punching bags, kid-sized "gerbil cages," balls of all shapes and sizes, an indoor batting cage, a soccer goal, a golf net, basketball hoops, an aerobic floor area, and even a putting green inspire his young customers to be active and develop their skills. "We're basically an intense PE function that supplements the public school offerings. Academics are dominating the school day and that is great. But our customers don't want PE cutbacks to negatively affect their child's growth." He continues, "Baby boomers grew up in schools known for strong PE and sports programs. They want that for their kids, too, and today's parents are willing to pay for it."

Johnson hires college student PE majors as his instructors. Because he can't pay these students much for their part-time work, he "compensates" them by improving their leadership skills. "They come out of here with a nice resume. I instill them with my enthusiasm and coaching skills, and that in turn gets passed directly to our young customers."

Johnson acknowledges that building his gym's membership took longer than planned. "I took a second mortgage on the house, borrowed from friends, family, and even 'Uncle MasterCard.' Things were very frightening for a guy who was used to a steady paycheck."

The gym helped make ends meet early on by renting its space to fencing, karate, and square dance clubs after its 9:00 PM closing. "Those partners kept me alive in the early years and we still have several groups involved that way." We even have some corporate parties come out for late evening retreats and team-building events. After hours rentals have been very, very good to me," Johnson says with a smile

Johnson's deep roots in the community didn't hurt either. He personally contacted thousands of people via emails, phone calls, and door knocking. He was guest on two local talk radio shows and one station had him as a recurring guest on their Sunday night call-in show. "One of my former players works at that radio station." Johnson admits. He attended dozens of baseball, soccer, softball and other youth events to hand out business cards and offer free "spot coaching" only if asked.

Johnson's innovative idea and tireless promotion are paying off. He seems pleased to announce that there are waiting lists for some of the more popular time slots. Johnson is contemplating the addition of another facility in another part of town.

Despite his slow start, Johnson is clearly enjoying life. He agrees enthusiastically by saying, "Full classes, kids, health, fun, and I get to be my own boss. How can life be any better?" Since giving up that regular paycheck, Johnson appears to relish his role as his own boss who is not accountable to the school administration or the community. It looks like Coach Johnson has scored himself yet one more winning touchdown.

Web Sites That Were Helpful to Joe:

www.pecentral.org
Premier web site for health and physical education teachers

www.aahperd.org
American Alliance for Health, Physical Education & Dance

www.pfit.org
Professional fitness instructor training organization

www.ncsf.org
National Council on Strength and Fitness—certification group

28

Learn Your Marketplace

Job-Jumping Banker "Goes Steady"

Thanks for asking me to speak to your MBA class tonight. As you know from my introduction, I don't have an advanced degree so I don't feel very comfortable speaking with you. But, perhaps we can all learn together this evening as we discuss careers. Thanks to Professor Olson for having me here.

A couple of years ago, I was fed up with the banking world. In only four years I quit one bank, got laid off from another, and went through two mergers. This was shocking since my parents both worked in the banking industry, uninterrupted for a combined total of nearly seventy years!

After college, my folks encouraged me to interview with large banks, feeling that they would be stable employers. I accepted a job with a large downtown bank and loved my role as a personal banker trainee. My personality and skills enabled me to progress quickly and I was soon allowed to make larger loans. I was promoted to a suburban branch.

Several co-workers became friends and I joined in the bank's sports leagues and employee clubs. My salary was not huge, but I appeared to be on the "fast track."

My second annual review came and I got a modest increase with lots of promises about my future. They promised to move me into small business lending or mortgage banking—two areas with higher income potential. With that encouragement, I got a more expensive apartment and bought a new, low-end Audi, much to the dismay of my parents.

Then the surprise merger hit. A large, national player "pooled interests" with us and all bets were off for my future. They still needed good staff to run the place, but everything took on a bureaucratic feel. Decisions were usually run past some off-site "Big Brother" manager.

Over a year passed, and I was given no new responsibilities. My third salary review was a joke. My old boss stated "there is a new sheriff in town." I didn't like the sheriff so I quit and joined another bank in town as a Small Business Lender Trainee.

I had over three years of experience yet they called me a trainee! But, I was just glad to be out of the old situation. What I quickly realized was that my new situation was similar to my old job! It seemed that the quality of work you do is not as important as the politics you play.

Dad and Mom never talked about this stuff when I was a kid. And yet their bank went through a merger shortly before I went to college. I brought this up at Thanksgiving and they admitted that they did have politics, but noted that mine were more pronounced. We agreed that this was most likely due to the fact that they worked in smaller towns and my workplace was a bigger city. They made the point that they experienced corporate politics but their family obligations forced them to shut up and get along. They were passing a message on to me that day and it came through loud and clear.

As unbelievable as sounds, my new bank ALSO experienced a merger. This time, we did the acquiring of a local bank system which was of a similar size to ours. Everyone expected some staff shuffling. My lending portfolio was flat in the next few months due to the "wait and see" merger confusion amongst our clients. The new entity eventually decided to close our facility as it was close to a nicer branch office of the company we had acquired. I assumed that I would be moving to our downtown office. Well, you know what they say about the word "assumed."

The new entity's strategic staffing planning group decided that there were too many people in my job classification. My layoff was justified because I was new at the bank, new to my field, and had not yet produced any noteworthy results. I couldn't argue with them on these issues. The kicker was that the "old-boy" rainmakers all stayed on board. I was bitter but moved on.

Here I was, at age 26, and stuck with an expensive car, a nice apartment, and no job! I could hear my folks quietly chanting: "We told you so." Fortunately, the bank gave me a "special situation" severance package since I had joined them just seven months previous. They threw me three months' worth of salary since they were unable to honor their previous commitments. I was encouraged to be very quiet about that deal.

I knew I wanted to avoid a bank job for my next position. However, my entire experience was in banking. The Farm Credit System needed more agricultural background than I had, so that was not an option. **I was adrift**. I applied for many jobs but got little response. I couldn't believe that I was pigeon-holed after only three years in one field!

After two months, I visited with a career coach to breathe some life into my job search. She helped me realize that many major employers in our city had internal credit unions, including educational and government entities. Suddenly I realized that I knew about one dozen plus new potential employers!

Most of these credit unions had little, if any turnover and none were advertising for new staff. My coach worked with me to devise a strategic approach. Some approaches involved a letter, some an email, some a phone call, and two included walk-ins. I tried all approaches and ended up with four separate interviews and two offers! I accepted the one at the insurance company's credit union as that looked like a very stable situation.

After just two years, I was moved into a lead lender position there. We moved into our own new building two months ago and it feels just like a branch office of one of my former banks. My boss told me that my youthful energy combined with my big-picture understanding of lending is what earned me the promotion. She is a great boss.

My career coach knew her stuff. She turned a negative into a positive and knew exactly where and how I should showcase my talents. My folks are thrilled, the future looks stable, and I got to keep my Audi! Life is good again and I plan to stay put for a long, long time.

Web Sites That Were Helpful to Jenny:

www.aba.com
American Bankers Association—trade group

www.cuna.org
Credit Union National Association—trade group

www.americasjobcoach.com
Career coaching company

www.abwahq.org
American Business Women's Association

www.workingwoman.com
Magazine for professional women

29

Be Open To Opportunities

Nurse Assistant Alice Offers Comfort

Jill,

With your background in sales and public relations, I hope you can give me some constructive criticism on the following letter. It is the latest draft of what I plan to use to "market" my services. I am not sure I need a letter at all because I am quite busy, but my husband thinks I should do this. What do you think?

I feel called to this kind of work and I have spent my life preparing for it. I never would have imagined that I could earn a living doing something that I love this much!

I ask folks to pay me whatever hourly rate they think is fair. This work ends up averaging out to a nice wage for me and it lets me do what I do best. This isn't about money-- although it is nice that I can serve critical patients without spending all that time on my feet. I am earning more than when I worked at the hospital and I now have great flexibility.

Laid Off & Loving It!

Is the following letter too long? I do want people to know my background, skills, and motivations for doing this kind of work. Thanks again for your input and editing. I appreciate your help!

Peace,

Alice

Here is the letter:

* * * * * * *

127

Laid Off & Loving It!

Dear Clergy Person,

      This letter is to introduce you to my services that I believe compliment yours. When families are involved in a medical crisis, you offer comfort to families and their loved ones. I also do that in my role as a professional visitor.

      For twenty-seven years, I worked in numerous Tennessee hospitals, clinics, and nursing homes as a (Certified) Nurse Assistant. I have worked beside doctors, nurses, and all other health-care professionals, with all types of patients in all types of patient settings. My work involved the hands-on patient care jobs with and for patients. Everyone tells me that I have the best bedside manner around. Two years ago I resigned because I was unable to keep performing the physical demands of the position.

      That is when I "fell into" my work as a professional visitor. A long-time friend named Margaret was admitted to the Intensive Care Unit. I stayed by her bed night and day until her West Coast family could finally arrive. Margaret's husband died long ago. Her family thanked me profusely for the time I had spent with my friend. I was glad I was there for her because Margaret died two weeks later.

      When I was keeping vigil over Margaret, I got to know some of the other families who were also in the ICU. During a visitor lounge chat, one family asked me to stay at their mother's bed side while they were forced to leave for a brief outside commitment. It struck me then that my ability to **be present** was my calling, my skill, and a needed service. I stayed with their mother for about two hours and I was happy to help. Upon their return, the family insisted on paying me for my time. I was embarrassed that they offered and promptly declined, much to the family's dismay.

      The word got out about me and one thing led to another so I now spend over thirty hours a week actively visiting

128

geriatric care facilities, intensive care units or hospitals for children. I love supporting children whose parents have to sneak away from their sick beds. Families are scattered all around the country these days, so they too seem to appreciate being able to engage me to be there for their aging parents until they can arrive.

I **never** act as a spiritual advisor to the patients or their families. Only when asked, will I read the books of faith provided by them or their families. The rest of the time, I read **Chicken** *Soup For the Soul* stories, newspapers, magazines, or just hold their hand. Sometimes I hum tunes that I think the patient might enjoy hearing.

I write to you simply to inform you of my availability should any of your parishioners ever need this service. My contact information is listed below. My services are offered on a donation only basis and I tell everyone this on the front end. Some people cannot offer anything and I am still happy to help anyway. I am not in this for the money but somehow I continue to earn a modest living at this avocation.

I have spent my whole career preparing for this kind of work and I love that I am able to offer this service. References are attached. Thank you for your time and attention.

A servant,

Alice Smith

Websites That Were Helpful To Alice:
www.frontlinepub.com
CNA Support Site
www.cna-network.org
Certified Nurse Assistants trade and service organization

www.hospicefoundation.org
Service organization to end-of-life patients

www.ncnafs.org
National Certified Nurse Assistant Friendship Society

www.chickensoup.com
Chicken Soup for the Soul web site

www.homeinstead.com
Non-medical elderly visiting service

30

Move On From Rejection

Major Mike Makes His Own Job

After 21 years of honorable service in the United States Air Force, I thought the private sector would scoop me up immediately. But after months of post-retirement job hunting, I was still unemployed. It seemed like the business world didn't know how to react to me. So, my job-hunting struggle turned me into an **employer**. This is my story:

My retirement came after a well-decorated career with USAF. At my peak, I had nearly 100 direct and indirect reports. I led Total Quality Management task forces, I supervised network technology professionals at two separate bases, I earned my MBA, and I was recognized for my work at a European staging base during Desert Storm. I had a stellar service record, proven management abilities, technical savvy, and strong linguist skills.

Still, I couldn't capture the attention of the hiring officials in the corporate sector. Some of my experience was specific to military settings, but I thought companies need good managers. I managed some very complex functions. During my few corporate interviews, the employers implied that most of their mangers were promoted from within. I only brought linguist work and specialized defense expertise to the table—not any internal company knowledge.

Fortunately, my military pension and Marilyn's good job allowed me a leisurely job search. I researched, studied, and researched some more. I got very good at spotting employment trends in the newspaper and online. A local meatpacking plant always had openings for production workers. Seeing that trend, I invited an ex-USAF friend to lunch. After his separation, Jerry landed a job as a programmer analyst with that company.

I drilled him on his take of the problem and he summed up in one word: "Turnover." He said that extremely high turnover amongst the laborers consistently slowed production and threatened quotas. Many of the production workers were of Hispanic background, and some key managers were Hispanic or spoke some Spanish. Still, Jerry said there was a climate of distrust, disconnection and dismay throughout the facility. Staff needs were ignored too often so rehiring and retraining kept the plant from operating as smoothly as it could.

The situation reminded me of a project I handled while in the Air Force. There our staff was constantly in flux due to the weekly arrival and departure of staff. Trust amongst the troops was low due to the slow acclimation and rapid turnover. New arrival training slowed productivity and there usually was a cultural adaptation issue due to the overseas location.

Back then, I was told to "fix the problem" and, after 'ten thousand' meetings, classes, interviews and new policies, we whipped that place into shape. I won strong recognition and praise for the increased morale and productivity.

As a result of this experience, I was convinced that I could improve the situation at this meatpacking plant. This confidence was also due to my Spanish linguist skills and my management history. I tapped my friend for all the information that he was comfortable giving to me.

I created a solution to what I thought the plant's problems were. I approached the proper person whose name I had obtained from my programmer friend. I requested five minutes of time to demonstrate to him a way that would increase his floor production. I had no background to make this kind of claim but figured I had nothing to loose. It took two weeks to actually catch him on the phone. He finally agreed to hear me because he was tired of deleting my messages off his voice mail! I left messages on his voice mail in both Spanish and English.

When I met with him, he told me that profit margins are always thin and that my consulting was "too expensive" and probably not needed. That's when I cleverly offered to perform work on a contingency basis. That got his attention since I wouldn't be paid unless my work brought something to his bottom line. Due to my internal reference check, professional conduct, and well-prepared handouts, he agreed to run my thoughts past his boss.

Two weeks passed, and the facility experienced a raid by the United States Immigration and Naturalization Service. Eleven illegal immigrants were working there without the proper documentation. The plant paid some fines for that. The company complies with immigration laws, but sometimes the there are a few paperwork forgeries that are hard to detect. When the firm earned less-than-flattering press, they decided to try something new. My timing now appeared to be perfect as I was told that they wanted to try some of human resources solutions.

My ideas were quite basic. I knew very little about the meatpacking industry, but I do understand how to build trust and get people work together. I simply served as a liaison, go-between type of person. I was not a manager of the plant nor was I a production worker, so both parties considered me "safe." I performed ombudsman roles to all concerned. The plant had bilingual staff and a good HR department, but I simply floated around the production areas, being more available than most of the other administrators could be. I sometimes hung out at management meetings too.

All I do is help all parties to communicate and be knowledgeable of the needs of the other group and that is paying off. Progress is slow but the word has gotten out that our plant is an OK place to work. It has taken six months to make any noticeable progress. Our workers are attracting their friends and relatives to come and work here and turnover has decreased remarkably. We still have problems, but the "hire-train-lose" cycle has slowed noticeably. The plant management now has me on a steady retainer. I am my own consulting company!

We all know the reason this works is that I am not an employee of the plant. My financial retainer is not huge, but on an annual basis it will be more than I grossed annually while working for Uncle Sam. It works for all of us.

And now I have become an employer. Instead of looking for a job, I am looking for employees. My attorney and accountant have me structured in an S Corporation (and helped me to acquire the proper types of insurance) so I can safely hire additional consultants. I became an employer because the parent company wants to try my formula in two other plants that they own. I have some prospective employee leads from my Air Force linguist connections, plus I have my eye on hiring talent right from our plant if management will allow that. I think they will.

I believe that I found my niche. Two years ago I would have never imagined that I'd go from the command center to "carcass central" but, I am now improving the lives of people, helping an employer be more profitable, and building my own corporate consulting practice.

Now, instead of listening to employers tell me why I didn't fit into their companies, I help employees to be productive in their own workplace.

Websites That Were Helpful to Mike:

www.americasjobcoach.com
Career coach to separating military personnel

www.pegasuscareers.com
Specialists in military personnel placement

www.nase.org
National Association for the Self Employed

www.latpro.com
Placement service for Spanish and Portuguese speakers

www.ehires.com
Permanent placement firm – technology focus

Appendix

Part 1: Twenty-Minute Career Tune-Up™

Part 2: Occupational Improvement Formula

Part 3: Affiliate Income Opportunities

Part 4: Americasjobcoach.com Services

Part 5: Getting **Your** Story Published With Us

Part 6: Who Is Paul David Madsen,
        ...America's Job Coach?

Appendix Part 1

Twenty-Minute Career Tune-Up™

"A Career Clinic"

Jobs, careers, and businesses occupy a great deal of our energy. If you work full-time, your job is where you invest most of your non-sleeping hours! Perhaps that is why we refer to them as "occupations." Few other activities in our lives occupy us so fully.

On the job, weeks turn into months and months turn into years, so it is wise to get a career tune-up now and then. It can keep you fresh and help you avoid a false sense of job security, and it may fine-tune your occupational marketability.

For those who are laid off and actively looking for gainful employment, the Twenty-Minute Career Tune-Up™ can move you more rapidly toward your goals.

For those who are not currently in a career crisis but who do wonder what else is out there for you, this tool may move you closer to your occupational PASSION--just like some of the people featured in *Laid Off & Loving It!*

Where has your occupational life led you? Take the Twenty-Minute Career Tune-Up ™ and find out! You deserve to get a snapshot of what is occupying you because...

...your time is your life!

Twenty-Minute Career Tune-Up™

This exercise will rush you through a big-picture look at your occupational life. Prolonged analysis of the questions will defeat the benefits of the brainstorming path. Fill in as many of each section's blanks as possible.

This exercise is helpful to job seekers and career changers, but also to small business start-ups that are trying to add new customers.

Section 1   Personal Inventory

List your *Personal* Assets below. Examples of your
PERSONAL assets may be "prompt" or, "pleasant" or
"efficient." Job-related assets come later so use this
exercise to describe your <u>personal</u> traits. Go!

_____   _____

_____   _____

_____   _____

_____   _____

_____   _____

_____   _____

_____   _____

_____   _____

_____   _____

_____   _____

**Now go back and circle the five traits that help
you feel "<u>successful</u>" as a person.**

Section 2   Professional Inventory

List your *professional* assets below. Use another sheet of paper if needed. Examples of your professional assets might be "skilled at XYZ," or, "results getter at...," or "highly diplomatic with..." Use just a few words or short phrases only—no long sentences. List many skills and job assets that enable you to successfully complete and perform your work. Can you fill up all of the blanks? Go!

_____   _____

_____   _____

_____   _____

_____   _____

_____   _____

_____   _____

_____   _____

_____   _____

Now *circle* the **five answers that are the most important for your "success" at work.** Which traits helped you get your job, help you keep your job, or allow you to excel in your work?

Next, *place a check mark* in front of the five skills you most enjoy using on a **day-to day basis.**

Section 3

Outstanding Occupational Accomplishments

List your most prominent **occupational accomplishments**. What stories or outcomes can you point to that really "define" your career? What "glory stories" capture the high points of your work? Team outcomes are fine but remember to focus on YOUR role and contribution to those successes. List a brief phrase that helps you refer to the event or outcome.

An example might be "I saved the Jones Account" or "I delivered a 21% profit in the Midwest territory after two years" or, "I taught Johnny to read after everybody else had given up." Come up with at least five examples. GO!!

1.

2.

3.

4.

5.

Section 4

Your Occupational "Summary"

List two of your top "success-oriented" personal traits (from Section 1):

1.

2.

List three of your "success-oriented" professional traits (from Section 2):

1.

2.

3.

List the top two skills that you most enjoy using on a regular basis:

1.

2.

List two assets, traits, or skills you utilized to achieve your 'Outstanding Occupational Accomplishments'

1.

2.

Continued...

Now combine your most successful personal and professional skills and attributes together with your best professional accomplishments to create an Occupational Summary. This summary "defines" **<u>your unique occupational self</u>** and your specific, most **marketable** strengths. Limit this summary to around 25 words or so, in two or three sentences. Create you own or customize the following open-ended templates to fit you:

*What I do is help_____ _____ to _____ _____

_____ _____ _____.

*I specialize in (increasing/assisting/reducing/helping/growing /teaching/leading/enabling)_____ _____ to_____ and _____ or _____.

*My (employers/clients/customers) thrive because I _____

_____ _____ _____ ___ _____

due to my proven _____ ___ _____

_____ _____.

*Due to my expertise in the_____ _____ _____ (industry/company/market/niche), I enable my (customers, employers, clients) to excel in their _____ because_____ _____ _____ and _____

_____.

continued...

Section 5

Bringing It Together –
Define Your Passioniche™

People thrive occupationally when they utilize their preferred skills, traits, and abilities in a forward-moving **environment**. Biological organisms are typically **growing** *or,* **they have begun to decline and degenerate.** <u>Careers and jobs can be like that.</u>

List the <u>TYPES</u> (not the names) of employers, industries, or customers that can benefit from your specific Occupational Summary (Section 4).

1.

2.

3.

4.

5.

6.

7.

8.

9.

10.

Congratulations!

You have just defined your Passioniche.™

You have summarized your combination of personal, professional, and 'favorite use' skills and applied them against the backdrop of an existing or a new industry market niche. It can serve as your occupational mission statement.

Combining your passion and your niche has created YOUR very own "Passioniche™**"**

Summarize your Passioniche here:

Appendix   Part 2

Occupational Improvement Formula

"The APTAC Solution"

After completing the Twenty-Minute Career Tune-Up™, you have a quick occupational road map of <u>what you like, what you have done well,</u> and *where* <u>you can apply those successes.</u>

The Occupational Improvement Formula (**APTAC Solution,** for short) involves five **specific** steps used by our coaching staff:

1. **Assessment. Learn where you are now. What is your Passioniche™?**

2. **Posturing. <u>Properly</u> presenting your background, skills and interests.**

3. **Targeting. What companies, customers, and employers need your services?**

4. **Approach. Define and make a strategic approach of your targets.**

5. **Closing. Close the deal, job offer, gig, negotiation or engagement.**

Completing your Twenty-Minute Career Tune-Up™ walked you through **Assessment, Posturing**, and **Targeting.** Parts 4 and 5, Approach and Closing are not included <u>inside</u> The Twenty-Minute Career Tune-Up because they take longer than twenty minutes!

The following is a road map of ways you **can** approach your targets. Be sure to contact Americas Job Coach for more ideas about **your** unique strategy!

Remember that several of the narratives in Laid Off & Loving IT! describe strategic employer, customer, and client approach techniques.

Keep checking back to <u>**www.AmericasJobCoach.com**</u>
for more info on the *APTAC Formula.*

<u>Strategies for Approaching New Employers or New Customers and Closing the Deal</u>

Targeted letters of inquiries

Mass mail letters of inquires

Targeted email inquiries

Mass email inquiries

Targeted faxes

Mass faxes

Cold telephone inquiries

Warm telephone inquiries

Get friends to introduce you

Get strangers to increase you

Trade association networking

Customer group networking

Mass/blanket networking

Career coach utilization

Headhunter utilization

Get noticed by the media

Market your services as a consultant/contractor

Develop a compelling Unique Selling Proposition

Develop a Unique and effective 'elevator speech'

Church/Synagogue and charity organization networking

Closing:

Ask for the job, gig, or engagement

Remind them through dedicated, creative follow-up about how they will benefit from YOUR service.

Remember to point out to them "what is in it for them."

The Closer's Rule: The *persistent* inherit the Earth!

**For more information on Approach Strategies,
contact** aptac@americasjobcoach.com

Appendix Part 3

Affiliate Income Opportunities
with AmericasJobCoach.com™

AmericasJobCoach.com™ offers our qualified affiliates the opportunity to earn supplemental income through our affiliate program. The current details of this program are updated often and described on the www.AmericasJobCoach.com web site.
The program simply revolves around the concept of our affiliates referring their friends and customers to us for mutual benefit. Commissions are earned when the referrals of our affiliates purchase media products, seminars, memberships, and coaching services.

Everyone knows someone who is interested in improving his or her occupational situation. Now you have the chance to help them and earn some supplemental income at the same time. We are accepting applications from representatives in most geographic locations.

IMPORTANT NOTE:
Affiliates of AmericasJobCoach.com are **NOT** employees of the company nor do they possess any authority to bind, attach, or officially represent us beyond the basic introduction of clients and customers. They are not franchisees, employees, investors, or owners. They simply introduce customers to our services for the benefit of all involved. To learn more please visit:

www.AmericasJobCoach.com
click on the "**income opportunities**" button.

Appendix Part 4

AmericasJobCoach.com Services

AmericasJobCoach.com adds value to your career/small business in the following ways:

1. Summits: Small group, career-enhancing seminars for professionals like you

2. Community Coaching: Large group seminars

3. One-on-One Coaching: Individual engagements

4. Media Units (books, ebooks, newsletters, ezines, Internet and broadcast talk shows)

5. Memberships: Individual enrollment that bundles the above services

6. Corporate Services: Enabling corporations to provide "soft landings" for key, separating employees

Services, continued…

Coaching is available on these and other career topics:

- Career Values Clarification & Assessment (numerous tools)

- Strategic Career Posturing Inside Your Industry or Niche (resumes and more)

- Strategic Potential Employer Targeting in Your Preferred Geographies (online and other tools)

- Strategic Employer Approach and Closing Techniques

- How to Tap Your "Insider" Hidden Job Market

- Independent Consultant Assessment -- Are You Ready?

- How To Succeed as an Independent Consultant— Marketing support

- Interview Preparation & Offer Negotiation Strategies

- Strategic Team Building and Recruitment Training

- How to find new profits that are "hidden" inside your present small business or small business idea

Contact Paul David Madsen with questions or comments:

paul@americasjobcoach.com

For our latest offerings and services visit:

www.americasjobcoach.com

Appendix Part 5

Author Submission Guidelines

AmericasJobCoach.com is actively soliciting original author stories for possible inclusion in our upcoming books, recordings, online or offline magazines, or newsletters. We seek stories from the **original** authors that demonstrate "success" in career and job transitions, and small business start-ups. We particularly love stories about the underdog who came out on top!

Stories from across the occupational spectrum are welcomed, and all submitted job or career-related stories will be considered. In the future, AmericasJobCoach.com MAY be in a position to pay original authors for the submissions that make it into our final printed or recorded products.

Payment terms, rules, and content theme needs change on a regular basis, so please watch for current information via the "author submissions" button on our web site:

www.americasjobcoach.com
"author submission information"

Benefits To Contributing Authors:

By having your story included in our subsequent books and recordings, you will gain exposure to *our* rapidly growing public. We will usually list bios of each contributor complete with your contact information, if you desire. You will be helping others to grow because future readers can learn from you! And, you will be **raising your own professional visibility**. We hope to hear your story!

Appendix Part 6

Who Is Americas Job Coach?

Paul David Madsen has been heavily involved in all facets of the employment services sector for 18 years. He has worked in key roles for two multi-billion dollar information-technology consulting corporations and several local and regional executive search, staffing, and placement companies. Some of Paul's career activities:

- Made over 18,000 headhunting, recruiting, sourcing, screening, and interviewing contacts with active and passive job seekers in numerous states and countries.
- Conducted over 21,000 sales calls and candidate presentations and approaches to hiring executives, managers and human resources professionals in nationwide corporations of all sizes
- Host of the weekly **America's Job Coach Radio Program** on Omaha, NE radio station KCRO (AM 660). Conduct "Career Repair On The Air®" with listeners from four states who call in for advice.
- Taught career transition courses to hundreds of professionals, early retirees, lay-off victims, and others for over eight years
- Placed hundreds of job seekers in new positions in many US locations
- Founder of Group One Associates, churchpros.com, ehires.com; and The Career Transition Institute
- Earned in 1987, the criteria for his Certified Personnel Consultant designation from the National Association of Personnel Services
- Is a long-time resident of Omaha, Nebraska where he lives with his family and is active in the community
- Is a graduate of Dana College in Blair, NE
- Author of a *Laid Off & Loving It!* and other upcoming books on occupational improvement

Check often with

www.AmericasJobCoach.com

<u>For:</u>

- **Seminar schedules**

- **New title releases**

- **Talk show schedules**

- **And the latest in tools you need to optimize YOUR occupational success!**

<u>Quick & Easy Order Form</u>

- Fax Orders: Send this form to 402-502-3399
- Phone Orders: Call 800-789-4769-have credit card ready
- Postal Order: Americas Job Coach 13520 Discovery Drive #Suite 221 Omaha, NE 68137
- (Online Order: www.AmericasJobCoach.com)

Please send the following product(s). I understand that I may return my purchases for a full refund, for any reason, no questions asked.

_____

Quantity (number of each item)_____

Please contact the indicated person regarding the **services** of AmericasJobCoach.com: _____

His /Her contact information:

Sales Tax: Add 6. 5% to the price of any products being shipped to a Nebraska address

Shipping By Air: US: Add $5.00 for the first book or recording and $2.00 for each additional product.

Payment: ____Cheque____Money Order (make out to ehires.com)

_____Credit Card Type: ____Visa _____ MasterCard ___Discover

Card
Number_____

Name On Card_____

Expiration Date: MM/YYYY_____

Ship Product(s) to: Include Name, Address, Zip Code, Phone (with area code), and email address: